ALL I NEED
POISE
TO KNOW
CLASS
I LEARNED
FROM MY
TEXAS
CHARACTER
DISCIPLINE
HIGH SCHOOL
FOOTBALL COACH
LOVE
PRIDE

A handbook of wisdom for parents, young people and yes, even coaches!

CHRIS DOELLE & KEN PURCELL

All I Need to Know I Learned from my Texas High
School Football Coach

by Chris Doelle & Ken Purcell

FOREWORD

by Dr. Charles Breithaupt

It is difficult to explain why football is so revered in Texas. It is much easier to show someone. More than 1,200 high schools play football in our state. Each Friday night in the fall, entire communities come together to watch teenagers from their local high school compete on the gridiron. But, it is much more than a game.

The participants on the field are the central figures of the contest, yet hundreds of other teens are involved through bands, drill teams, cheerleaders, flag corps, drum lines and booster clubs. The congregation of all of these groups brings about a sense of what is right in Texas. Families and friends gathering together to celebrate the lives of our youth make for an eventful evening. The key to making it all happen is the high school football coach.

Chris Doelle paints a great picture of the influence the high school coach has on young lives in *All I Need To Know I Learned From My Texas High School Football Coach*. He has effectively utilized the knowledge and passion of Coach Ken Purcell to describe the value of these experiences. These authors capture the essence of this thing called football and the coaches who lead.

Both Chris and Ken understand the passion the game requires. Football is not easy. It is a tough game played by tough kids. Those kids are lead by men who believe that football is a microcosm of society. Developing character, learning to deal with adversity, understanding how to deal with aches and pains, becoming trustworthy and dealing with success are just some of the attributes for which coaches must provide guidance.

This book shows how coaches think and what they value. The authors hold coaches in high esteem because they know that often times that coach is the last influence before many students hit the streets. More often than not the coach is the surrogate parent. The coach is the standard bearer for what is right in the eyes of many athletes.

Every coach in Texas understands the awesome responsibility of coaching a high school team. We have been playing football in Texas since 1892. During those 125 years we have learned that the coach holds the key to the development of young people through this great game. They also know that coaches are held to a higher standard. They realize the game of football demands more than simply physical development.

Throughout this book we learn the thoughts and processes coaches utilize to reach teenagers. We are able to see how great the opportunities are for these young men as they utilize football as a tool to becoming better adult men.

Football is not for everyone. But, football to those who participate, can be life changing. Coaches understand the magnetism of the game. They apply motivational techniques and sophisticated strategies to enable their teams to become successful on and off the field.

The drama of a Friday night football game in Texas is one of the most rewarding experiences we can find in our state. Watching how coaches orchestrate game plans and provide outlets for success through all of the pageantry of a football game is incomparable. I can't adequately explain it. But, Chris Doelle and Ken Purcell have done a great job in *All I Need To Know I Learned From My Texas High School Football Coach*. I highly recommend it to all who love the game.

Dr. Charles Breithaupt
Executive Director
University Interscholastic League

CHRIS DOELLE

I was never a star athlete that made the headlines. Yes, I was fast. I could run, but I wasn't large. (As a high school Senior I weighed 135lbs) What I excelled at was not quitting. No matter the sport, I would be the last one on the field or court. Endurance was my gift.

I used that gift to excel at bicycling long distances and to outlast my more explosive opponents. Sure, they could out-jump and out-muscle me when a game started but by the fourth quarter, they were sucking wind and I was still plugging along at the same pace I started.

In addition to having great endurance, I was a student of the game and more importantly, a student of the players. I found I could see things... "tells" that opponents would unknowingly give that I could use to my advantage. What fascinated me as much as finding an angle to win a game though was watching how the coaches got athletes to perform. That developed into a love of psychology - a love which led to my psychology focus in college.

I have used what is spelled out in this book not only to win games and motivate teammates or athletes I am coaching, but coworkers, friends, family and more. This stuff applies to so much more than who has the most points at the end of a sporting event. These values, habits and teachings are invaluable in the most important game... the game of life.

I have often told people that if there is anything good in my actions or beliefs it is because of my mother. She taught me things like "if you can't say something nice, don't say anything" and countless other bits of wisdom. After having a conversation with her last year and telling her how often I give her credit for my development, her response was the genesis of this book.

"You give me a lot of credit, but I think your high school football coach had a lot more to do with who you became than I did," she said.

Don't misunderstand, I think she was just being modest but she did open my eyes to the impact that football and particularly the coaches had in my life. It was that simple statement that finally put into words what it was I loved about Texas high school football. It wasn't about the band, the grass, the plays, the concession stand or the crowd - things I thought was at the core of my love for the sport. It was what Texas high school football means in the grand scheme of life... it was love.

After a decidedly average high school football career, I kept my connection to football in a variety of ways. I was a player/coach at the intramural level as well as an official for area high school games. I continued

officiating after college and added coaching at the youth football level as well. In 2004, just a few months after podcasting was invented, I created Lone Star Gridiron. This was only the 5th podcast in existence making it the first sports podcast, first football podcast and of course, first Texas high school football show. Within the first year, the website that served as the home for the show grew into one of the top sites and is now considered the authority on Texas high school football.

In 2015, while attending the annual Coaching School put on by the Texas High School Coaches Association, I was killing time between meeting coaches by sitting in on a FOX Sports Southwest Press Conference. It was there that I first heard Ken Purcell speak. I could instantly tell that he "got it." I decided right then and there that I had to talk with him and that his voice would be a perfect fit for the audience we had built over the last 13 years at Lone Star Gridiron. He was preaching to the choir and I knew we would be a great fit.

Just a few shows into our run, it dawned on me that Coach Purcell was the missing piece to a puzzle I had been working on for quite some time. I knew I wanted to put together a book explaining my love for and belief in Texas high school football. As we discussed the values Coach Purcell taught his staff and students, it was exactly what I was starting to put together in the book. Just as instantly as the decision to speak with him back at Coaching School, I blurted out "Coach, we should write a book together!"

You are reading that book.

Learned from Coach - Doelle/Purcell

KEN PURCELL

My first involvement with Texas High School Football was in the fall of 1962. I was a freshman in high school. I had great speed for a freshman so

8

the Head Football Coach, Lynn Hulsey, put me on the Varsity kickoff return. In the second Varsity game of that season I returned a kickoff 99 yards for a touchdown and I was in love with the game. Now, 54 years later, I still love the game.

As an assistant football coach, Head Football Coach, and Athletic Director for 41 years, I preached the values learned while playing Texas high school football. Many coaches that I worked with over the years often said to me, "Coach you need to write a book"! I always replied, "I am not an author!"

That brings me to July 26th, 2015 San Antonio, Texas. I had just finished a Press Conference for Fox Sports Southwest. I was leaving the hotel ballroom when Chris Doelle said, "Coach Purcell have you got a minute?"

Chris introduced himself and asked if I would be willing to do a weekly segment on his Texas high school football program. The opportunity dovetailed with my weekly on air work for Fox Sports Southwest, so I said yes. After our seventh weekly show, Chris said, "Coach we should write a book"

I laughed and said, "I have heard that many times before," and told him the same as always, "I am not an author!"

He quickly said, "I am," and so, here we are!

Texas high school football is the greatest game on earth - not just for the excitement of the game, but for the valuable lessons taught through the game. Hopefully, this book supplies wisdom, knowledge, goals, and common sense to use while "coaching" young men and women. It should provide insight into teaching, discipline, pride, poise, class, accountability, and decision making that a person can use the rest of their lives. And finally, it demonstrates that, *All I Need to Know I Learned from my Texas High School Football Coach*

TODAY'S WORLD

First we must acknowledge that the title of the book was inspired by Robert Fulgham's book *"All I Really Need to Know I Learned in Kindergarten."* That book, a runaway bestseller published in 1989, referred to the basic lessons that every child was taught in kindergarten. It was full of advice like - share, play fair and clean up your own mess. Fulgham's wisdom was easy to see.

What many missed however, was why it was such a great success. People craved this simple advice because society was already fracturing and the slide down the slippery slope was picking up speed. That was nearly 30 years ago and society has since crashed off the edge. Rather than being taught to play fair and clean up your own mess, our kindergartners are being taught to gender identify as whatever they feel like. They are being taught to stifle their freedom of speech. They are being taught that to say the right thing is better than doing the right thing. They are being taught that being 'cool' is more important than being nice. Rather than learning how to think... they are being taught what to think.

The first edition of this book is scheduled to be released in the fall of 2017 and society is much different than it was just a few years back - much less a few decades ago. When we were growing up, things were quite a bit different than they are today. The summer was a break from school, but not from work. It was the time when kids spent most of their free time outside. Also, growing up in rural Texas, most of the jobs available to teenagers were outside as well.

We loaded pipe and dug ditches. We hauled hay and loaded feed. Hauling hay isn't even a thing anymore. Now you see the huge round bales that are created by a machine and loaded by a machine.

Hauling hay "back in the the day."

Hauling hay today

Oh, and we did our hay hauling and physical labor jobs in between our two-a-day practices.

Two-a-day football practice is still in effect around the state, but it is a lot different now. When we were kids, you woke up at 6am, ate breakfast and walked out to the end of the road to catch the athletics bus. On-board, you headed off to the morning session of practice. It was a physical practice that involved wind sprints, bear crawls and the dreaded bus tires - running in full pads holding a bus tire above your head as you sprinted from one end zone to the other. If the tire touched your shoulder pads, you had to start over. When you returned, it was a quick lunch and then off to work. Often times, that work was hard, manual labor. If you were lucky, you would get a short break before heading off to the late session of two-a-days. It was brutal, but it taught us that our bodies were capable of much more than we suspected.

It is different today. Young athletes head to two-a-days when their chauffeur mom or dad drives them to practice... or they drive themselves. Another ride home often ends with eating in front of the TV or XBox. It is there they sit until it is time to repeat with the late session. These kids are capable of just as much effort, just not required.

Don't get me wrong, I know there are still kids today that have to work and still those that spend the in-between hours being productive and yes... even being outside. The issue is not with them, it is with that mythical 'average' teenager. Things have changed for a great many of them and not just in how they spend their summers. These changes are societal and because of that, today's teenagers are growing up in a completely different world.

An article popularized by Paul Harvey (but actually written by Lee Pitts) was reflective of an earlier time in our society and unfortunately rarely seen these days. It is only in places like the world of Texas high school football these are still taught.

"We tried so hard to make things better for our kids that we might have made them worse. For my grandchildren, I'd like better.

I'd really like for them to know about hand-me-down clothes and homemade ice cream and leftover meatloaf sandwiches.

I hope they learn humility by being humiliated, and learn honesty by being cheated. I hope they learn to make their beds and mow the lawn and wash the car.

I really hope nobody gives you a brand new car when you are sixteen. I hope you have a job by then.

It will be good if at least one time you can see a baby calf born and your old dog put to sleep.

I hope you have to share a bedroom with your younger brother. It's all right to draw a line down the middle of the room.

When you want to see a Disney movie and your little brother wants to tag along, I hope you'll let him.

I hope you have to walk uphill to school with your friends and that you live in a town where you can do it safely.

I hope you learn to dig in the dirt and read books. When you learn to use computers, I hope you also learn to add and subtract in your head.

I hope you get razzed by your friends when you have your first crush on a girl, and when you talk back to your mother that you learn what Ivory soap tastes like.

May you skin your knee climbing a mountain, burn your hand on a stove and get your tongue stuck on a frozen flagpole.

I sure hope you make time to sit on a porch with your grandpa and go fishing with your uncle. May you feel sorrow at a funeral and the joy of holidays.

I hope your mother punishes you for throwing a baseball through a window and that she hugs and kisses you when you give her a plaster of paris mold of your hand.

These things I wish for you -- tough times and

disappointment, hard work and above all, happiness."
-- Paul Harvey

Instead of sending you out into the world hoping you will skin a knee and learn lessons only taught by experience, now our kids are coddled, protected and sheltered. They are also over-chauffeured, over-scheduled and over-entertained. They are growing up in a world that is completely different and very foreign to that of their parents and grandparents. It is scary in some respects yet not scary enough in others.

Today's World:

1. We now live in a world of litigation.
2. We now live in a world where no one wants to be accountable, but everyone wants to hold everyone else accountable.
3. We now live in a world where everything must be documented.
4. We now live in a world where authority is continually questioned.
5. We now live in a world where everyone wants and expects a winner.
6. We now live in a world where humble, gracious and positive athletic role models are hard to find.

Today's Student-Athlete:

1. Student-athletes are much wiser today. You can't fool them.
2. Student-athletes have more athletic choices today.
3. Student-athletes have more personal knowledge of their sport today.
4. Student-athletes have fewer stable home environments today.
5. Student-athletes are part of our commercial work force today.

Today's Parent:

1. Today's parent is younger than ever and possesses fewer parenting skills.

2. Today's parents expect professionalism from their coaches.
3. Today's parent runs select leagues and athletic camps.
4. Today's parent has a different set of values from the past.
5. Some of today's parents will use technology to check a coach's driving records, criminal records and personal information, and then make the records public.

Today's Head Coach:

1. Today's Head Coach must understand their legal rights and obligations.
2. Today's Head Coach must welcome "accountability."
3. Today's Head Coach must nurture and give direction to their assistant coaches.
4. Today's Head Coach must have a "philosophy."
5. Today's Head Coach must not view coaching as a job, but as a commitment to student-athletes.
6. Today's Head Coach must learn to "document" events.
7. Today's Head Coach must sell their program.
8. Today's Head Coach must be a role model whether they want to be or not.

Today's society is all about "rights and privileges." Athletics however, is about "obligations and responsibilities." The trend of "everybody plays, everybody wins" has the short-term goal of boosting Johnny's self-esteem but the long-term effect of discounting the work and effort that go into improving oneself. It is in this effort that character is forged. It is in this effort that people become accountable to themselves and others. It is in this effort that young men of character are developed. "Participation" trophies are not only worthless, but teach our kids exactly the wrong lessons. If you want a trophy, you should earn it through hard work, perseverance, teamwork and yes... even luck. Life is not fair and winning doesn't always go to the best player or even the hardest worker. It sounds harsh but it is a valuable lesson.

Giving a child a trophy without having really earned it misses a great opportunity to teach lessons about not only hard work, but about disappointment and frustration. This experience will make it easier when they don't get into the college they wanted or miss out on that promotion. By awarding trophies to everyone, you rob them of extremely valuable life

lessons.

Too many parents in an attempt to protect their children, rob them of these learning and growing opportunities. Rather than helping your child to become resilient, you teach them to be fragile and train them to have trouble dealing with setbacks. Parenting is not about swaddling your child in emotional bubble wrap. It is about helping them grow into strong, resilient adults that can do the same for their children.

The family unit used to provide a lot of that character development and growth, but forces in society have decimated the family. This family is needed now more than ever. You have divorce rates through the roof because everything in society teach young men and women not to stick through things - not to work hard at things like relationships but to be selfish and to put their needs and wants ahead of their spouse. Only by continually putting your spouse ahead of yourself does a marriage work. It is a give and take. At times a husband needs to put his wife's needs ahead of his and at times she will need to put him first. As long as both focus on what is best for the other, not only does a marriage work, but it flourishes. It is under these circumstances that it thrives and becomes a source of growth and learning for the children involved.

Again, don't jump to the conclusion that it is our stance that there are no good marriages anymore. If your mind is heading in that direction, you are most likely reading this bent on finding fault. There are great marriages still despite the pressure from society. There are parents who do an amazing job in transforming their children into valuable contributors to this world. What is undeniable however, is that they are getting fewer and further between.

It is not just the family that is under attack. Football itself is under attack and it's got a lot to do with the liberal media. Liberals don't like football...they don't like tradition...they don't like traditional things. And they want to put down traditional things and of course in Texas, there's nothing more traditional than Texas high school football. They use the stories about things like concussions as evidence of why we should do away with football; but according to many reports football is behind things like bicycles and skateboards for the number of concussions per participant. What values are taught on bicycles and skateboards?

These are some of today's realities and this book will speak to each of these segments. It will show how athletics and Texas high school football in particular provide a much-needed source of development for today's youth.

WHY FOOTBALL?

First the case for sports in general. You hear mixed reports of whether or not athletics is good or bad for kids. The pro-athletics groups claim:

- 95% of CEOs played sports in high school.
- GPAs of student-athletes are higher than non athletes
- Pregnancy rates of female student-athletes is lower than non athletes
- The average budget for sports is less than 2% of total school budget yet creates revenue
- More than 50 years after high school, people who played high school sports still demonstrate more leadership, self respect, self-confidence than people who were not part of high school sports

But, there are groups hell-bent on removing athletics from society because they see it as a barbaric opportunity to teach people to dominate others and teach competition instead of cooperation. They claim:

- Team sports participants demonstrate "less/lower" character compared to individual sports participants
- Females demonstrate "more/higher" character compared to males
- Non-athletes demonstrate "more/higher" character when

19

compared to athletes.

So what is right? As the saying goes, there are "lies, damn lies and statistics." The point is that studies are put out showing anything a political agenda is set on proving so we will discount all of these studies and rely on first hand experience. With our combined experience over 75 years, we have seen that a) athletics can be very positive if combined with a great coach and b) football is head and shoulders above other sports when it comes to teaching the most important life values.

Football is one of the last arenas in America where men can be men and be praised for it. Football in and of itself if not what makes you a man. It does however contain within it all the ingredients to help a boy become a man. It doesn't apologize for the harshness. It doesn't shy away from contact. It rewards young men who are willing to enter the fray unsure of the outcome. It punishes those who take it lightly or too timidly. There are no shortcuts in football. Football is all about hard work and the sweat equity that you put into it, and many of its lessons aren't fully realized until years after you've handed in your pads for the last time.

This isn't about a player becoming a better linebacker, it's about a young man without ambition or goals becoming focused. It's about a kid seeing himself as a college student. Its about a selfish teenager deciding to put others ahead of himself. Its about creating young men of worth that will continue to do things on the 'good' side of the balance sheet.

"Football is just life marked off in 100 yards."
-Bill Badgett

Yes, you can learn a lot of life lessons from many sports.By pointing out or focusing just on football, we're not trying to demean any of them. There is just something special about football. Football is different than other sports in several ways. Football is the sport in which teamwork is essential to success. In basketball, you can run an isolation play for the star player. In baseball, a star pitcher can control a game, but in football, if all eleven players don't do their jobs on every play you have very little chance of winning.

As far as I know, its the only sport where you can play an entire game, an entire season - an entire career without touching the ball. Think about that. In every other sport (volleyball, basketball, baseball, water polo...) you touch the ball at some point. Even if you are one of the "lesser" players you are called on to touch the ball.

But in football, that's not the case. A lineman - if he's lucky, at some point in his career (maybe on a fumble) falls on the ball. In a crazy circumstance he picks up the ball and runs. Rarely do you have those guys touch the ball. So big deal, right? He doesn't' touch the ball... Well, it is a big deal.

That fact probably teaches one of the most important lessons you get from this game - selflessness. It teaches you that to succeed you do so as a team. That victory isn't about selfishness. Victory is about teamwork. And it teaches you to put others ahead of yourself. That lineman works hard to make a hole for his running back, protect his quarterback or beat the player in front of him. When they win a game - a district title or a state championship do you think their joy, their celebration is any less than that of the kid who scored three touchdowns? No. Because that kid doesn't score at all without that lineman's help.

Also, a quarterback, running back or receiver knows he doesn't gain a yard or score a point without the lineman doing his job. Each of them is dependent on the other to do their part.

A lot of the things attributed to football are applicable to a lot of sports. Even though we have interactions, knowledge of, dealing with other sports - football has it all. And for that reason this book will be written from the standpoint of football.

Does every Texas high school football program get it right? No. It is not perfect and becoming a football coach in a Texas high school does not instantly transform a poor motivator, mentor or communicator into a great one. The majority of these programs and coaches teach the right things. But yes, there are some turds in anything. In society however, we are tempted to throw the baby out with the bathwater when we hear a negative story - don't do that.

Texas high school football is one of the last bastions of conservative values available to our youth. It is one of the last places they can learn discipline, pride, accountability, perseverance and a self-image creating belief in their own possibilities. And for that reason, it needs to be maintained, protected and promoted.

But football is just for great athletes

This idea couldn't be any further from the truth. In fact, most football programs (including those in Texas) are made up of a wide range of athletic ability. What separates a winning program from a losing program (and thus a winning young man from a loser) is not whether they are athletically gifted. It is in those qualities taught by Texas high school football that require absolutely no physical talent, that a winner is born:

Positive Things that Take Zero Talent

1. Effort
2. Passion
3. Attitude
4. Showing up
5. Being on time
6. Work ethic
7. Body language
8. Energy
9. Being coachable
10. Doing extra
11. Being prepared
12. Not quitting

Also, there are no shortcuts in football. Football is all about hard work and the sweat you put into it. Many of its greatest lessons aren't fully realized until years after you've hung up your helmet for the last time. General Raymond T. Odierno, Chief of Staff of the U.S. Army, credits football for getting him into West Point, and cites leadership and fitness as the two qualities most sought after in military recruits. Football teaches the heck out of those qualities. In the life of former Texas high school football players, their playing time is a very short time. The impact they attribute to football lasts a lifetime.

GOOD COACHES

Anyone who has participated in sports for any length of time has likely come across bad coaches, average coaches and great coaches. It is important to point out that in our experience from pee wee football on through to connections with college and pro coaches, football seems to have a higher share of great coaches.

Good coaches have a lot in common and those commonalities are the result of good programs.It could also be argued that good programs are the result of good coaches. Good coaches hand down the lessons and expertise learned from their early mentors to those young coaches coming up in their program. In Texas, this wisdom is sacrosanct and treated as the Holy Grail of a winning football program. This knowledge has been passed on, refined and added to for over 100 years.

"Coaches don't win football games. Players win football games. Coaches win players."
-- Unknown

Philosophies Of Effective Coaching

1. Coaches must be role models in both Academics and Athletics.
2. Kids don't love the sport the way we do.
3. Kids don't care how much you know, until they know how much you care.

4. You get one chance to make that first impression.
5. You and your team will seldom exceed your own expectations. Set them high!
6. Coaches can and should be campus leaders.
7. No negative situation deters us or our programs.
8. We "respond" to situations instead of "react."
9. People can't see a difference in our actions or approaches to our players, parents or community whether our teams are winning or losing.
10. Athletics is microcosm of real life.
11. We coach co-curricular activities, not extra-curricular activities.
12. We praise the performer and criticize the performance.
13. We are professional educators and professional coaches.
14. Athletics teaches valuable lifetime skills and disciplines that are not taught in the academic classrooms.

Good Coaches Philosophy Of Practice

1. Be properly dressed out and on time for all practices. If you don't do it, you can't expect it.
2. Don't relax during calisthenics, stretching and warm-up. If its important enough to do, it is important enough to do right.
3. Time is the only thing all competitors have in common. We must use our time to the fullest. Have equipment and drills ready.
4. Give attention to all players on the team. Don't let anyone go unnoticed.
5. Go through the locker room after workouts. Stop and visit. Let the kids see you as a person.
6. Do not allow things to lay around the dressing rooms. Everything has its proper place. Attention to detail wins ball games.
7. Don't go home right after a workout. Some of the best game plan adjustments are made following workouts.
8. Do not accept anything less that perfection. Practice does not make perfect. Perfect practice makes perfect.
9. Hustle - enthusiasm breeds enthusiasm.
10. Have daily practice goals. Goals should be both short range and long range.
11. Keep your poise and confidence on the field at all times. It will

transmit to your players.
12. Give your players "little secrets" to help them.
13. When you get tired, pray for strength.

Some of these items may seem silly if you didn't grow up in this environment, but they are so very important. As you can see, coaching is not about barking orders from the sidelines (although that certainly happens.) It is more about teaching by example and being that "father figure."

Whether that influence is unavailable to these young athletes or in addition to the positive role models they currently have, it is invaluable. Sometimes hearing the exact same lessons of their parents, but from an outside source, makes the difference between a child taking it to heart or blowing it off as something "my folks gripe about." Even more important is that for many, this is the first time someone outside of their family has shown a belief in them. With that belief comes an expectation that a player has to fulfill. Expecting great things of someone is a powerful motivator.

Ways to Recognize a Good Football Program

When you look at the things that separate a good football program from even an average one, there are some things that stand out.

How they respond to adversity - We all have trying times and if you haven't experienced any, you are a liar or not very old. A good program looks very similar regardless of what is on the scoreboard. Their body language doesn't give anything away. You don't see helmets tossed to the carpet when they give up a score. You don't suddenly hear the language get louder or bluer. When a player fumbles the ball or tosses an interception, does he slump his shoulders and hang his head or does he keep moving and keep doing the job? The same thing is true (and more important) of the coaches. If they respond poorly - too high or too low - the kids pick that up. It begins and ends with the head coach and is filtered from him to his assistants and the athletes.

They don't make silly penalties - Every team will have penalties... some earned and others not. The ones we are talking about here are the unnecessary ones. Being lined up offsides, too many players on the field, unsportsmanlike conduct and the like are the ones that good programs just don't commit. The difference in the outcome of a football game can hinge on the tiniest of mental (or emotional) errors so it is important to make sure they don't happen.

Emotions are in check - This dove-tails into the response to adversity, but it also covers how a team deals with good things. Football is chock full of ups and downs and getting extremely emotional for either, can not only sap a lot of energy that could go into playing better football but it devalues real emotion about really important things. A good program keeps those emotions in check and because of that the players have the security of knowing how their coaches will react in situations. When the sidelines get out of control, the ability to win a game does as well.

They protect the ball - This seems so obvious because everyone knows you can't win if you don't protect the ball but there is a decided difference between good programs and others in how they deal with things like loose balls. Good teams do NOT try to scoop-and-score you see in the highlight reels when the ball is on the field. They fall on it. PERIOD... end of story. They don't high-step into the endzone holding the ball out. They don't get creative and try pitch backs. They trust in the system and if a play looks as though it is going to be shut down, they go down. Sure, they fight for all the yardage they can, but they do so with both hands covering the ball tightly.

They get the most out of players - In high school football a program gets what it gets. Sure, there are move-ins and a winning program attracts parents that have more mobile careers, but the bulk of your team is just a matter of who grew up in your area. Without an exception the top programs have a system that begins in junior high and often even the pee wee level. This gives coaches more years to see a player and help them develop to fit a position but still the program must fit these players' skill sets. Top programs will adjust their game plans each year to fit the athletes they have. If you have a mobile quarterback that is as capable as running the ball as throwing a strike 30 yards down field, it is easy. The next year when you have a QB that is better standing in the pocket - or maybe can't pass much at all, you adjust the game plan.

They are confident - The difference between winning and losing is often times simply a belief that you are going to win. When two evenly matched teams or players face off, the confident (not cocky) one usually comes out on top. Strong programs install confidence in the players and staff and that is directly reflected in their on-field performance. When a player feels secure in what is he going to do, the less confident player picks up on that and immediately falls into a reaction posture. When you have more of your players dictating action and their players reacting, you win. The great thing about this is it becomes a self fulfilling cycle that continues to build confidence in the confident ones.

They are tough - You don't see soft teams win games. You don't see soft coaches field winning teams. You don't see soft programs build or keep winning coaches. The players on good programs have a physicality that just isn't there in a weaker program. You see it in the game, on the practice field and in their lives long past football. If you want a great program, you have to have toughness.

They take care of little things - When you look at programs that are consistently at the top of their game, everything about them is top-notch... *especially* the small stuff. Little things like paying attention when a coach is talking. Little things like picking up the wrist tape you just ripped off after the game instead of leaving it lay on the locker room floor. Little things like responding, "Yes, Sir" or "Yes, Ma'am" instead of "uh-huh" or just nodding your head. Little things like making sure the spelling of names on the roster is correct. Little things like the hand shake at the end of a game. Little things like starting and ending a practice on time. Little things all add up to the BIG things in a program's success and cannot be overlooked.

Good football programs are not entirely caused by a single good coach but impossible without them. Good programs are a reflection on a good coach sharing his values and belief with the assistant coaches, teachers, players, parents, administrators and community. It takes all of them to succeed but it begins with a good coach. Legendary Texas high school football coach Chuck Moser explained this of why his teams were so good.

"We had 800 kids playing football in 18 elementary schools scattered around town. And eventually they all came to

Abilene High. The reason our kids were good was because they wanted to be good."

Coach Moser won 49 straight games as head coach of Abilene from 1955-1957. His modesty aside, Abilene and other schools with great programs accomplish that because they run a good program. Success breeds success and winning is merely a side-effect of either a strong coach building a strong program or when a new coach is needed, a strong program seeking out a strong coach to keep the ship headed in the right direction.

To be a good coach, you need to be clear on what is expected. It must be specific. You must give kids the *secret* stuff, don't try to coach generalities. You've got to tell them exactly what you want step-by-step, teach them how to do it and instill in them your's and the program's expectations.

At the beginning of a new season, Coach Purcell would hand out a two-part flier showing what the coaches would expect from the players and what the players could expect of the coaches. It makes it very clear to the player that there will indeed be things expected of them. But it also assures them that they can count on the coach to live up to what is listed as well.

What is Expected of the Football Team

We expect you to do something worthwhile with your life. We expect you to have great expectations. Anticipate having a great day, a great practice, a great season and a great life. We expect the following things from you:

To get an education
To give your total effort
To give unselfish love and respect to your teammates
To practice to the best of your ability
To be totally honest in all your dealings
To be extremely proud of your school, administration, teachers, coaches, teammates, family, friends and most importantly yourself
To be prompt
To be courteous
To display traits of good self-esteem

To be emotional and enthusiastic

What is Expected of the Coach

To respect you as an individual and never verbally or physically
        abuse you

To be loyal and honest to you in all areas of accomplishment and
        failure

To teach you that problems are a constant part of life and attack them
        as challenges

To provide the leadership and training necessary to set and achieve
        goals

To assist you in any way possible, now and after you graduate

To make all decisions predicated on what is best for the team and
        then what is best for the individual

To give you discipline and teach you how to develop *self*-discipline

To teach you to exhibit poise in difficult situations

To separate the performance from the performer

To praise the performer and criticize the performance

To teach you some football skills along the way

These list are more than just words in tables. They are the lifeblood
of what turns an athletic endeavor into something greater. It is the difference
between a program that puts 'win at all costs' and one that puts 'the
betterment of the kids' as the primary goal. You can win a few games with a
good Xs and Os coach, but you can't change lives and develop men of
character if the Xs and Os are all that matters. Because this belief is
ingrained in the fiber and history is one of the reasons Texas stand apart
when it comes to high school football.

WHY IS TEXAS DIFFERENT?

A lot has been said about the braggadocio of Texans. Let's get some of those out of the way first:

"What you northerners never appreciate ... is that Texas is so big that you can live your life within its limits and never give a damn about what anyone in Boston or San Francisco thinks."
-- James Michener

"Don't Mess With Texas"
-- Texas Department of Transportation

"That's why I like Texans so much. They took a great failure and turned it into a tourist destination that makes them millions. Texans don't bury their failures. They get inspired by them."
-- Robert Kiyosaki (on the Alamo)

"You may all go to Hell, and I will go to Texas."
-- Davy Crockett

"The miracle of Texas lies in the fact that it is the work of a

handful of men. In not a single fight during the entire period from 1800 to 1845 did they muster as many as one thousand fighting men. Overwhelming odds never discouraged them and defeat but spurred them to ultimate victory."
-- Jack Butterfield

"I'd rather be a fencepost in Texas, than the king of Tennessee."
-- Anonymous

"Texans ignore "better," long ago forgot the useless word "good." Everything in Texas is "best."
-- Edward Smith

"Always marry a woman from Texas. No matter how tough things get, she's seen tougher."
-- Dan Rather

"If a mans from Texas, he'll tell you. If not, why embarrass him by asking?"
-- John Gunther

A lot of our state pride seems excessive to outsiders. They consider it brash, boastful and rude. The problem with that conclusion is that most of the claims in which Texans take such great pride are true. Texas was built on the backs and blood of a rugged individualistic breed of settlers. The Republic of Texas was carved out of the cactus, rattlesnakes, scorpions, oppressive heat and bloody battles between Indians, Mexicans, and a half dozen countries that fought over these lands.

Because Texas came through all of this, Texans have an innate "can do" attitude that more often than not proves to be true. We were bred to face obstacles because its "what we do." That mindset has passed on from generation to generation across the kitchen table, in the fields and as parents put their kids to sleep at night. With the attack and subsequent breakup of the family, Texas coaches are sometimes the only place this thinking is taught anymore. It is alive and well on the high school football field.

When you see so many former Texas high school football players among the NCAA and NFL elite, it's not that we have stronger athletes or faster athletes; It's just that we have better coaches. Again, don't take this as just Texan bragging. Coaches from all over the country acknowledge that the absolute best coaches are in Texas. In other states, you can work at a tire shop or insurance company until 5 o'clock in the afternoon, then go coach the high school football team. Here in Texas, coaches are educators. You've got to have a teaching degree. You have to be an educator before you can coach. That's the big difference but its not the only one.

In Texas, coaching football is a profession, but it is even more than that... it's a calling. The following list has been making the rounds on social media and is very applicable to Texas high school football coaches.

What Coaching Isn't

Coaching is not... Something you do, it's something you are.

Coaching is not... A 'punch the time clock' job. It has no set hours.

Coaching is not... About egos, personal glory or agendas. It's about serving others.

Coaching is not... A job you get with the sole focus of making money. It is more about outcomes than income.

Coaching is not... About what's best for you. It's about what's best for the athlete and team.

Coaching is not... All about championships and silverware. It's about 'people care.'

Coaching is not... All about the Xs & Os. It's about the Ps & Ss (people and standards.)

Coaching is not... About the destination. It's about the journey and lessons learned along the way.

Coaching is not... About you. It's about others and those you coach.

Coaching is not... A job.It's a vocation and a calling.

In other states, an athlete sees his football coach after school for an hour or so. In Texas, we have an athletics period as well as practice after school. We have tutorial periods during which students work on any areas of their school work where he is falling behind. Often times, that same coach is the kid's math, science, history or English teacher as well. This amounts to a lot of influence, motivation and inspiration opportunities for that coach. When you add to that, the assistant coaches who are teachers, mentors and tutors also, you have a core of people around the young athlete that care about his success in life, not just on the field.

Another big difference for Texas high school coaches is the opportunity and desire to work together to help each other become better. Associations like the Texas High School Coaches Association (THSCA) put on events year round to educate, fellowship and help Texas high school coaches constantly improve and grow. Each year in the summer, THSCA puts on Coaching School. It is a multi-day event that provides countless lectures aimed at improving coaches in the state. Another great benefit of these events is the opportunity to strengthen the brotherhood that exists between these coaches. That too, ensures that a shared set of values remain among Texas high school coaches.

VALUES TAUGHT BY FOOTBALL

First off, let me say that a lot of what we will cover in terms of values apply to most team sports but as spelled out in the Why Football? section, football does it all just a little bit better. These are lifelong traits that will not only be useful in winning games, but in winning the game of life. These skills will be used in facing adversity on the job, in relationships and more. They will be reflected in the character of the athletes as they grow.

The other thing that needs to be pointed out is that it is NOT a guarantee. Coaches, parents, teammates and sports programs play a role in instilling these values, but it isn't 100%. Again, the chance that athletes will adopt these values goes up greatly in Texas because the coaches are professionals and teachers. What a kid does with the information is still up to him. You know the old saying, "you can lead a horse to water, but you can't make him drink." Texas high school football players drink that water more often than not because they see and learn the benefits of doing so, but at times some athletes miss these messages.

Also, you can pick up some of these values without a good coach, but the odds go way down. Parents can teach these principals and young people can even develop them without a good role model. It just makes it that much easier when you have a program designed to teach values and coaches who view the development of young people as a calling rather than just a job.

First, let's take a 30,000 foot view of the values and principles taught through Texas high school football. Each of these will be broken down into its own chapter.

Hard Work is putting in the effort necessary to not only play your role on the team, but to make the team better. It is coupled with the perseverance to not quit or give up before the job is done.

Discipline is essential to any successful life. Our student-athletes will hopefully use the discipline that they have acquired while competing in high school athletics for the rest of their adult life.

Pride deals with self-esteem. Every student-athlete should develop a strong sense of self-esteem. Strong self-esteem is an attribute that allows a successful individual to give openly to others.

Poise is the ability to deal with adversity in a positive manner. During adulthood, we all deal with adversity. However, it is the manner in which we deal with that adversity that is truly important.

Class is a term used for how an individual deals with success and failure. Hopefully, our student-athletes learn to deal with failure and success in very similar ways. Class means that we are humble in victory and gracious in defeat.

Teamwork is not just playing the same game at the same time as someone else, but really working together to achieve more than you could individually.

Accountability for an individual's performance is a hallmark of athletics. Through athletics the student-athlete is held accountable for his or her performance. Win or lose, there are no excuses.

Decision Making is constant in athletic performance. Decisions are made on the court or field in a split second. The student-athlete cannot "second guess" those decisions. In today's society fewer and fewer people want to be responsible for making decisions. Through athletics we teach the art of decision making.

Leadership is showing others the right thing to do by action rather than demand.

Athletics is a microcosm of real life. That's the value of athletics in Texas high school football. If kids get to see a glimpse of what it's going to be like in their adult life, they won't be freaked out when the bumps appear in their road ahead. If they are actively taught these values, as they are in Texas high school football, they will be well prepared not only to deal with surprises that come up but to plan ahead to avoid them altogether.

HARD WORK

If you read any resume or CV, you will see "hard working" or "highly motivated" listed as attributes for the potential candidate well over 90% of the time. That is an example of what is known as "illusory superiority." The best example of which is that roughly 75% of people consider themselves to have "above average" intelligence. Let that sink in.

Hard work is a bit different in that it is a subjective thing. So, perhaps they all do feel they work hard. How does football figure into this? No, football is not the only place to learn the value of hard work, but it is a darn good one. Football is full of countless stories of people who succeeded simply by being willing to outwork others. Hollywood loves to tell that story via football. Some great examples are:

Rudy
My All-American
The Blind Side
Remember the Titans
We Are Marshall
The Junction Boys
Friday Night Lights

Also, the NFL and NCAA football ranks are loaded with examples of undersized athletes that overcame "expert's" opinions of their future prospects by being willing to outwork their teammates and opponents. Hard work is about more than just the underdog story. It is a vital part of the success of every single player on the team. Nobody gets far in football without working hard. It is a hard sport. It will tax a player physically as well as mentally.

It is hard to go to practice every day. It is hard to go full speed through drills. It is hard to put in the reps in the weight room. It is hard to keep your grades up so you don't lose eligibility. It is hard to put off hanging out with friends. It is hard to skip the junk food in favor of something more nutritious. It is hard to show up for film study on a Saturday morning after getting home at 1am from a road game. It is hard to keep your teammates fired up when you are feeling horrible yourself. It is hard to dig deep inside to find the strength to stand when every part of you is screaming to stay down and give up.

"No one has ever drowned in sweat."
- Lou Holtz

In a world where people grab Google for a quick answer to everything and look for any shortcut to avoid paying the dues in the life, reaching long-term hard-fought goals can seem nearly impossible. When you are forged in the furnace of hard work, life goals are no different than weight lifting goals, practice goals etc. When you have experience putting in the work to learn and grow incrementally, seemingly insurmountable tasks are possible.

President Kennedy said it very well when giving his speech at Rice stadium in Houston. He explained why the United States was taking on such a daunting series of tasks in the space program,

"...not because they are easy, but because they are hard, because that goal will serve to organize and measure the best of our energies and skills, because that challenge is one that we are willing to accept, one we are unwilling to postpone, and one which we intend to win."
- John F. Kennedy

No, he wasn't speaking about football but he may as well have been.

38

Football is taken on because it is hard. It is played because it will measure young men, coaches, schools, programs and more. Again, it is played with the intention of winning not because it is easy, but because it is hard.

Practice

That said, practice and hard work are not the same thing. A lot of people think that to become an "expert" or "elite" at something all you need is practice. In his book, *Outliers: The Story of Success,* pop psychology author Malcolm Gladwell famously claimed that 10,000 hours (roughly 7 years) of "deliberate practice" was enough to make someone world class in anything. While it sounds good, sells books and is a great tidbit to have at your disposal when someone you are teaching is whining about practice, recent research by Princeton University has shown it just isn't true. The study found that, on average, practice accounts for just 12% of the difference in performance and that depending on the field, it varies wildly.

- In games, practice made for a 26% difference
- In music, it was a 21% difference
- In sports, an 18% difference
- In education, a 4% difference
- In professions, just a 1% difference

When confronted with the lack of evidence for his claims, Gladwell responded with this:

"There is a lot of confusion about the 10,000 hour rule that I talk about in Outliers. It doesn't apply to sports. And practice isn't a SUFFICIENT condition for success. I could play chess for 100 years and I'll never be a grandmaster. The point is simply that natural ability requires a huge investment of time in order to be made manifest. Unfortunately, sometimes complex ideas get oversimplified in translation."
- Malcolm Gladwell

The first thing this tells us, is that it doesn't apply in sports. Let's look at that. Does that mean we shouldn't practice in sports? Not at all. People do not get better at anything without practice and people generally improve at something when they do practice. This study is just pointing out that practice alone isn't the key. So how does this tie into hard work? Doesn't it imply that hard work is not necessary? Not at all.

Practice is incredibly valuable because it isolates an activity. Muscle memory (myelination) is what is responsible for most of the gains from practice. Our body is a wired machine. Those synapses that fired the first time you walked were not very strong so you wobbled as a baby. The more you tried to walk (practiced) the more your brain learned which muscle fibers to fire, for how long, and in what order. Now, you walk without thinking about it. It is in making actions automatic that you benefit from practice. This is the reason why football coaches will have skill players carry a football with them day and night - to hard wire the act of holding onto a football.

But it isn't just doing a task over and over that makes you better at it. It is in perfecting a task that a person improves in sports.

> *"Practice does not make perfect. Only perfect practice makes perfect."*
> - Vince Lombardi

The legendary Packers coach said it well and that is where the hard work comes in. You can show up for practice and "mail it in" for the repetitions without much gain in skill. It is only when you work hard to make sure your form is correct, you are going full speed when needed, make sharp cuts, etc. that you get the true benefit of practice. That kind of precision and dedication to getting the most out of your reps and your God-given skills, requires hard work but yields results that will assist you throughout life.

When you have a culture of hard work, the limits you place on yourself just disappear. If you've never sweated through a t-shirt, if you've never walked out of the practice field just drenched in sweat, whether it's as a player or as a coach, then you have missed out. You missed out a tremendous experience in life. Through exhaustion, you emit endorphins. These endorphins are like superchargers to your system. Once you've experienced real sweat from physical effort, it changes you. You come out of it realizing that you won't die if you aren't carrying your water bottle on a walk with you. You will in fact, be able to answer the call when required to do something others consider difficult.

Perseverance

The flip side of hard work is perseverance. Texas high school football and perseverance go hand in hand. This is a hard sport. It is more than just hard. It is a brutal and taxing sport. Many people who don't understand it, wonder why anyone would put themselves through all that this sport requires. You learn perseverance from the very start because when you first take to the field, there is someone ahead of you already playing the position you want. It would be easy to just quit and say, "I can't be quarterback so why bother?" Those are not the kind of people football attracts and if one does happen to slip through, they get weeded out pretty darn fast. You have to persevere each and every single day in practice as you run drills over and over.

One of the main factors in kids' learning perseverance is honesty. When a coach is honest with them. and expects them to be honest with themselves, their path doesn't look as daunting. That open communication and trust of the people around you, build your faith in sticking with something difficult. With that faith, Texas high school football players are on their way to many personal victories. With that, you learn you can:

- Finish what you start
- Get back up when knocked down
- Play through the whistle
- Play through the end of the game

What about when a player is ready to quit but there is still more to do? That is when coaches and players suck it up and finish the job. This is what we teach in athletics, this is what we teach in life. We finish the job that we set out to do. So Friday night we play for the program, we play for our teammates, for our parents, for the school, for ourselves and for the community. And that's all we got left to play for.

Coach Purcell tells a touching story about a kid he coached. This kid was a dedicated player. The team had just missed the playoffs but had one game left in the season. They could have decided there was no point in worrying about the final game since they weren't going to the playoffs. This kid came in on Thursday night for team meeting and said "Coach, I've got a poem. Can I read it to the team?" His dad had written the poem and this kid was so moved that he wanted to share it with his teammates.

"High school football, you love it so, and when it's over, this is what you know.
You gave your best, you fought the fight, but half must lose each Friday night.
The memory of who won will quickly fade, but what you learn from the game you'll take to your grave.
And so my son, play the best that you can and be proud of the game that helped make you a man."

There was not a dry eye in the dressing room after he read it and the team went out and won what would be the final football game of the season. The game didn't matter in the playoff picture, but it meant a lot to most of those seniors for whom this be their final football game ever.

Losing is a great teacher

We spend a lot of time talking about the positives associated with Texas high school football, but what about the negatives? What about when things don't go your way as a player? What about when you miss that tackle or lose that game? Is there any way to see that as a good thing? Yes!

In today's society, we try to protect our kids from pain and struggle but that may be doing them a great disservice. More lessons are taught in the things that don't go well than are ever learned with smooth sailing. It is a fact that among the nearly 2,000 or so high schools in Texas half of them are going to lose a game each and every Friday night. That is a lot of losing! Trying to protect our children from adversity does them a grave disservice. Give your child the honor of learning from losing.

"Good timber does not grow with ease: The stronger wind,

the stronger trees"
-- Douglas Malloch

People observe you closer and learn more about you after a loss than after a win. After winning a game it's fun, you walk across that field and shake the opponent's hands; you pat your buddy on the back. But when you lose, especially for a coach (and the leaders of the team) you have a bunch of kids you need to take care of. Those kids need someone to hug their neck, speak some encouraging words and show them that you care more about them than you do about the outcome of a football game. That's the *secret sauce* of a really good coach. Those are the coaches that have grown men all over this state and beyond saying, "He was like a father to me." It is in the crucible of tough times that perseverance is either developed or crushed, and this game can do either depending on who is running the show.

DISCIPLINE

A lot of people confuse discipline with heavy-handiness or dictatorial leadership. That is not at all what is meant by discipline. Kids are not slaves to be forced to obey orders and follow instruction. It may sound corny, but they are our future. Discipline does not involve creating drones that follow in lock-step and obey without question. Discipline is about creating someone who can think for himself and has intestinal fortitude. It is about having the courage and wisdom to do the right thing even if it is hard and foregoing the easy way out. This is one of the biggest benefits acquired from playing Texas high school football.

According to a study by the University of Montreal, "By time they reached the fourth grade, kids who played structured sports were identifiably better at following instructions and remaining focused in the classroom. There is something specific to the sporting environment -- perhaps the unique sense of belonging to a team to a special group with a common goal -- that appears to help kids understand the importance of respecting the rules and honoring responsibilities." This is the value of discipline.

Discipline is developed by much more than just the coach, but he is a huge factor. During practice, the coach's role is multi-fold. First, he must instruct and demonstrate the physical movements, but much more is gained from the mental coaching. He is in a unique position to impact the athlete, potentially even more than parents and teachers. During what is a physically stressful time, the coach demonstrates the value of focus, teamwork, and delayed gratification. Having these and other values reinforced during a stressful period, the lessons become much more deeply ingrained than simply reading the same thing in a book or hearing someone in a lecture.

Another big benefit of learning on the practice field is the speed of feedback. This feedback is often instant which integrates the learning that much faster. In the classroom setting, the gap between effort and report card is often much too long for the benefit of reinforcement. In football, when you work hard during the week, it shows up during the game that weekend. That feedback loop trains the athletes of the importance of discipline. The discipline of working hard during the week is rewarded with improved results.

For a lot of first time football players, this is the first time in their lives they are learning to behave for themselves. It is not about criticism or punishment. It is about teaching them self-control. It is about this coach being firm, respectful and matter-of-fact with them. It is often also the first time they are treated as mature enough to be trusted to do things. This level of trust is a large reason why so many football players step up to the challenge.

People generally will rise up and step in to fill a void. By leaving that void for a player, a coach gives them an opportunity they may not get anywhere else. It is an opportunity to start taking responsibility for his own actions and live up to higher expectations about his capabilities. It is really quite magical to watch.

Even the best parent can use the exact same words, expectations and motivation often with a much less successful outcome. It is not because the parent is lacking in any way. It is simply because they are the parent. In football, the coach becomes a secondary (or even sometimes primary) father figure, but with a couple secret weapons.

1. He gets to build discipline around a sport that the child loves to play
2. He has the added weapon of the kids peers (this is huge)
3. He has some built-in authority without the baggage of all the arguments a child has had with parents over cleaning room, brushing teeth etc. It's a clean slate

"Discipline is a constant battle between your future self, and your present self. Do not let your present self short cut

and find the easy way to do things and ruin the visions and plans you have lain out for your future self."
-- Brick Haley

The coach may get all the credit for creating a disciplined young man, but most of it is internal. He is often just the catalyst that adds the right amount of motivation and the right amount of butt-chewing to cause the athlete to turn on his God-given self-discipline. A child will transform from a slacker that has to be pushed to any task, to one that chooses to set goals, achieve them and continue to do so.

This too becomes a self-fulfilling loop that joins goal setting and action with the rewards of achievement in such a way that it drives *more* goal setting and action. All of this growth is happening in an extremely palatable way because it happens without a conscious decision on their part and while taking part in an activity that they love. Why else would you play a game in which every player is hurting after it ends?

If you spend any time in a game or in practice, you will get hurt. Understand I am saying *hurt* not injured. This sport hurts. What is it that makes a player get back up after he is driven into the ground with a facemask full of grass and mud? It isn't how great it feels - that's for sure. It is discipline. You do not hear the coaches calling each player by name after each play and telling them get back up and go to the huddle. You don't hear them shouting to each and every player what they should do on the next play. It is the discipline of that player that stands him back up, and sends him back to huddle instead of home to a warm bath. It is his discipline that kept him showing up at practice so he understands what is expected on the next play.

Coaches come up with the schemes. Coaches do a hundred little things each week to give players the tools they need. But, it is those players out on the field running the plays. It is the discipline that *they* have turned on, that keeps them working together toward a goal.

Discipline is at the very core of why football is able to deliver so many values and experiences that former players remember for the rest of their lives. Discipline is the cornerstone upon which everything else that is great about football is built. Because this sport activates discipline so well, is why football is so much more than just a sport.

It's also no coincidence that discipline and disciple come from the same root word. A disciple is a follower of a teacher, philosopher or belief. As young men learn the values taught in Texas high school football, they too become disciples. They become disciples of the beliefs taught to them by these coaches. Among these beliefs are that you should do what you say you will. You should stand up for what is right and fight against what is wrong. You should defend those who need defense and attack those who would hurt innocents. You should stand as an example of your belief system. You should reap the reward of your efforts and pay the price for your transgressions. These are just a few of the beliefs that veterans of Texas high school football follow.

PRIDE

Pride is derided by many in society today, but allow us to make a case for it. We are not talking about selfish pride or vanity. We are not talking about foolish pride. We are not talking about arrogance. We are talking about acknowledging that you did something well and not shrinking from it because you were told modesty is always best.

"I cannot agree with those who rank modesty among the virtues. It is as much a departure from the truth to underestimate oneself as it is to exaggerate one's power"
-- Sherlock Holmes

No, pride is not always a bad thing. As we mentioned earlier in the book, Texas is quite at home with pride. Texas high school football instills a lot of pride and not in a bragging way. The old adage, "it ain't braggin' if it's true" comes to mind. It is our contention that there are two kinds of pride and they should be understood before going any further.

Sinful pride is boastful and self-centered. It is evident when you take credit for everything you are and everything you do. It discounts the involvement or assistance of others. It is putting oneself as the creator of all things good in your life and ignoring those who helped you. In naming yourself the creator, you are even discounting God in your belief that you can do it all. The Bible warns throughout of pride.

"Pride goeth before destruction, and an haughty spirit before a fall. Better it is to be of an humble spirit with the lowly, than to divide the spoil with the proud"
--Proverbs 16: 18-19

But there is also a good pride that is overlooked often. In fact, although all anyone ever seems to remember being mentioned about pride in the Bible is the sinful stuff, the Bible talks about this good pride as well.

"But let every man prove his own work, and then shall he have rejoicing in himself alone, and not in another"
-- Galatians 6:4

This is the type of pride we are talking about. It is okay to be proud of work completed in the course of something positive. It is okay to feel that swell of emotion in your chest when you gave your all in an effort. No, football is not solving world peace, but it is okay to take pride in the many good things brought about in this setting. It is okay to feel joy after helping a friend. It is good that doing good things gives you "warm fuzzies." That is pride. That is good pride.

Texas high school football has the power not only to transform the lives of the players but entire communities. We have seen countless times over the 125+ years of Texas high school football when a town or city comes together around a football team. It builds bonds unlike anything else. When community members take pride in something together it can be amazing to watch. You see run-down parts of town fixed up. You see attendance at community events increase. You see crime rates drop. You see graduation rates increase. You see neighbors talking and smiling with neighbors they never would have met, much less became friends.

You also see pride have dramatic effects on the kids. The most shy and reserved kid that doesn't look like he will be able to hold himself up, much less play football, transforms with the pride of being able to accomplish goals. Sometimes it is the quiet giant that doubts himself that comes out of his shell when he realizes he is capable of much more than he imagined. This pride is a great thing to witness. There is nothing negative about it.

POISE

Poise has been described as "grace under pressure." It implies self-confidence and maintaining composure during stressful situations. It can be as simple as staying calm in a traffic jam, being polite to someone who has just slighted you in some way, or even remaining focused in an emergency. As an example: We could be taking a road trip along the highway somewhere in the middle of deep West Texas. We could be chatting for hours, laughing, sharing heartaches, singing along with the radio or complaining about politicians. We spin out and roll the vehicle into the ditch and you will learn more about me in the 10 seconds following that accident than you did in the first four hours of that long drive. You will see how I handle adversity. You will see if I have poise or if I lose my head.

Poise is taught in Texas high school football each time something unexpected comes up. And that happens in every single game. There's two minutes left in the game, and you have the ball with a 3 point lead. You simply need to run the ball, run out the clock and win. Suddenly the running back fumbles and the other team picks it up running it into the end zone. Just like that you are losing by 4. That is when poise comes in.

You can't curse, toss your helmet aside and throw up your hands. There is nothing to be gained from losing your cool. It won't help the situation and will likely make it worse. The offense needs to get ready because now you've got a minute and a half to drive the length of the field and score.

Every position in football teaches poise as every position has someone that is trying to stop them from accomplishing their plan. Think of the defensive lineman whose job it is to run in and sack the ball carrier behind the line. There is an offensive lineman across from him who has a plan to stop that from happening. Within a fraction of a second after the ball is snapped, that defensive lineman's plan is under assault. Should he get mad? Start cussing? Just quit? Of course not. He has trained for this. He knows that he cannot control what the other guy is going to do, so adjusts his plan quickly and without unnecessary emotion. Does it always work? Nope, most the time it doesn't. In fact, out of the 100+ plays in the game there are usually only a few sacks per team - often, none. And at no time did any player know exactly what was going to happen on the next play. That is a whole lot of practice dealing with stressful situations and practice maintaining poise.

"The key to winning is poise under stress."
-- Paul Brown

Poise is more than just not losing your head. It is a quiet confidence when facing an obstacle. You see teams that get all fired up, scream and shout, do a dance, play loud music - anything to get them stoked and ready for the game. You also see teams that stand tall, face their opponent and exude faith that they are better prepared and better able to handle any situation that comes up. That can scream louder than any boom box. Confidence that you have done the work and are secure in the plan can be the difference between winning and losing. Every play ever drawn up is designed to make a touchdown. The difference comes down to who has a better plan and who executes that plan. Staying focused and executing the plan is poise.

How does this happen? How do coaches suddenly take emotional teens charged with hormones and get them to not lose their minds and their cool for a three hour football game? Practice is for much more than just learning plays.

- **Repetition develops skills.** The more reps a player has in practice that simulate game situations, the better able he is to deal with things that come up. As the skill fundamentals become second nature, the mind is freed to find solutions to situations because the body performs those skills on autopilot.

51

- **Concentration.** When coaches see a player losing focus in practice they correct it by teaching them to learn from the mistake, put it behind them and get it right. Staying in the moment also allows the player to better deal with the unexpected.
- **Breathing.** Coaches teach things with repetition because it helps in so many areas. If a player has done the same move 1,000 times, the breathing is the same and it too becomes second nature. Being consistent stops the unexpected from taking the breath away and causing things to speed up emotionally.
- **Confidence**. With consistent reinforcement that a coach trusts in their abilities, the athlete gains confidence in himself. This confidence is instrumental in maintaining poise during tense situations.

By the time a player graduates from high school they may have played in over 200 games (going back to junior high, pee wee etc.) If they were in for 1/4 of the plays during that span, we are still talking about over 5,000 plays and tens of thousands of reps in practice. That will build confidence and that confidence will manifest itself in poise during stressful situations.

As a grown man, they will have the chance to display that poise.It might be in an unfortunate situation. It might be in a car wreck that you're kids are involved in. It might be in a divorce situation. You must have the poise to keep your head and to think logically and do the right thing. This sport teaches that.

that's Chapter 1 of the story. Chapter 2 is I went immediately to
us and stepped on the bus. My kids know that when the coach
bus they quiet down. But I said, "Guys I wanna tell you that you
ng great tonight."

of course they were thinking about the district championship and
"Look out the window of this bus and see that man in there? Let
what he just told me about you," and I repeated what he told me.
aid "You've done two great things, you won a district
ship and you also showed me great class tonight."

xamples of class are even more evident when players or coaches are
sing side of the scoreboard. Sure, everyone is upset when they lose
py when they win. But the mature ones show class in victory or
That is a major theme taught by Texas high school football coaches.
e all seen reports and videos of coaches losing their cool when things
o well. (Some of you are old enough to remember Indiana basketball
Bobby Knight or tennis player John McEnroe.) Those stories make
ws, but you don't see things like that often in the world of Texas high
l football. When they do, they are dealt with swiftly.

If a coach loses his cool, how can he expect his players to show
? He can't. Things go poorly for both teams in every single game. What
rates the classy programs from the average ones is how they deal with
e missteps. Classy players don't blame others for mistakes. They don't
dirty tactics to "get back" at opponents who beat them on a previous play.
ey acknowledge they were beat and determine to do better. They often
n congratulate their opponent for a good move.

Football provides many situations coaches can use as opportunities to
ach and reinforce their lessons about class.

CLASS

"Class is an aura of confidence that is being sure without being cocky. Class has nothing to do with money. Class never runs scared. It is self-discipline and self-knowledge. It's the sure-footedness that comes with having proved you can meet life."

-- Ann Landers

First let's define what class is. It is style, manners, intelligence, the people you surround yourself with, the books you read, the movies you watch, how you handle either good or bad events. But is it more than that. It is is treating everyone with dignity and respect regardless of your relationship with them. Class is working to be the best you can and doing the best you can for yourself and others.

"Class never tries to build itself up by tearing others down."
-- Rudyard Kipling

Great football coaches teach class and make it an integral part of their program. Really, the game of football, with the smashing of bodies together at high speed, teaches class? This book isn't about just what is learned in the act of playing football. This is another area where coaches teach by example.

Athletes are taught class while playing football not only through the obvious things - helping an opponent up after a tackle or retrieving the ball and bringing it to the referee after in incomplete pass out of bounds. It also teaches class through literally thousands of acts of kindness a player witnesses in and around the game.

- A coach that lends an ear to a student (even if he/she is not on the team)
- A player that pulls a younger one aside to help with his technique
- The students that show up on Saturday morning to clean the stadium
- The car that honks and waves as they pass the bus on the way to a road game
- The football parents who run the concession booth at games
- The treats left for the players in their lockers
- Friends and family lined up along the road to cheer the bus as it heads out to a playoff game
- The players visiting the elementary school to high-five the kids
- Booster club fundraising events like auctions or "meet the team" nights
- A post-game hug that is just as long and tight whether it was a win or a loss

It is much more than those outward things. Players receive daily reminders that they have the great privilege of playing a sport they love, and with that comes a responsibility to live up to and honor the game. As a player you are taught to give back to your community. You are taught that people look up to you, not because it is so special to be a football player. Instead, they look up to you because you take on the duty of being a role model and kindness is a big part of that.

Texas high school football programs are very high on service. Community service. School service. Service to your teammates. It is very important to build teamwork and to build class in an organization. Whether you are helping your community or helping a teammate, it is always rewarding. Often times the reward is far greater for the one delivering service than for the receiver. Take the time to volunteer and help your

community.

"Unexpected, undeserved, unr(kindness change lives ... every undeniable.
-- Bill Curry

"Yes, Sir" and "Yes, Ma'am" are not about s you are in any way "less than" them. It is not about superiority. It is simply about respect. This is one of diminishing in society and is nearly extinct. It is howe Texas high school football. If you think it is corny or c welcome to that opinion. Just understand you are wrong

Texas high school football coaches teach players be kind. They teach kids to hold the door for someone (e. to say "thank you", "you're welcome" and "please." In sor Varsity football players even remain back in the cafeteria a up the area after the lunch period. It is not seen as corny, o demeaning. It is a great example of performing a kindness f(Performing an act of kindness is a sign of class.

In an interview on Lone Star Gridiron, Coach Purcell of class, "Class as I described to my kids is win, lose, or draw across the field, we shake hands with the opponent, we look th(and we say 'good job.' And if we got beat, we still do that. We s(We're going to have class in everything we do, the way we dress get on and off the bus."

"I won a district championship one time in Denison, Texas at a little steak house. My kids were loading on the charter bus afte and I was up there making sure that the coordinator paid the bill rig(manager walked up to me."

He said "Coach I need to tell you something about your team. I said "Yes Sir?"

The manager said, "Your kids did not mess up my bathrooms. 7 didn't get the salt and pepper and loosen the tops. We have had teams th. come in here and almost destroyed our place.

He added, "I know you won a district championship tonight, I just want to tell you that you got a great group of kids".

TEAMWORK

In life we are faced with hard times. There are moments when we are tested and long ordeals that will challenge us to the core. It is because this happens in real life that the lessons taught by high school football are so important. How we respond to these situations will make all the difference not only in that exact moment we are challenged, but will carry on to affect not only our entire life but the lives of those around us.

In football, we face challenges. That is the very nature of the game. Whether it is as simple as the challenge of moving a funny shaped ball ten yards in four attempts, or as daunting as dealing with a death of someone close to you, the ability to cope with, learn from and overcome tragedy is a muscle that is strengthened by teamwork.

An obstacle, challenge or tragedy can either bring people together or shatter relationships and teams into nothing. The difference comes down to a few key factors:

- Has the team experienced working together to overcome obstacles or achieve goals?
- Have they been coached that these setbacks are normal?
- Do they have an expectation of being able to succeed together?
- Do they believe in each other?

Teamwork is built by working together to overcome shared challenges. There is a bond in working in unison with teammates through the same exhausting practices and games. The physical demands improve your fitness. The mental demands strengthen your resolve. And the shared experience build a steadfast loyalty. Some of these demands may seem insignificant in retrospect but the roots of greatness are in each of these tiny hurdles. Here is just a small sampling of the challenges that Texas high school football teams face all the time:

- Practice is hard and requires effort
- Learning plays is not only a lot of memorization, but it is a totally new language
- 11 players on each side of the ball must learn the timing and communication to perform a play in concert
- There are 11 players on the other side of the ball doing their best to foil your plans on every single play
- The ball is shaped funny so bounces are very unpredictable
- Your teammates make mistakes that affect your results
- The demands of family life add extra stress
- Increased time demands make it difficult to get enough rest
- Officials often make calls that do not help your progress
- The clock sometimes works against you
- The fans sometimes work against you
- The lighting/sun/glare/heat/cold and other conditions work against you
- The crowd/band noise sometimes work against you
- Injuries work against you

There are a thousand little things that conspire to spoil your plan to get a first down, score or win a game. This doesn't even touch on REAL tragedies. Tragedies are inevitable but how we deal with them is not. Teams without much of a foundation can crumble and come apart at the seams when one strikes. Teams that are forged in the teamwork of thousands of tiny tests can come together, toss aside any small differences and create a bond that will not only last a lifetime, but serve each member long after the cleats are hung up for the final time.

Our real lives are lived outside of the world of football. Although athletes may feel like their sports is a huge part of their life, for most of them, it is a tiny blip. Four years playing high school football can seem insignificant to a 50 year old reflecting back on his life. It is uncanny though how many former Texas high school football players attribute that tiny blip as some of the most formative times of their lives.

"Talent wins games, but teamwork and intelligence wins championships."
-- Michael Jordan

But teamwork is much more than dealing with hard times. It is about success as well. Football drills into us that individual glory is secondary to what we can accomplish when working together. But, what does that mean?

It means that yes, you can score a touchdown or be carried off on the shoulder of your teammates after grabbing the interception that sealed the game and that is great. It is tiny though compared to something like beating a rival or winning a state championship... something that truly requires everyone to work together. You forget that touchdown you scored as it diminishes over time, but you never forget victories you had as a team. Yes, in football, but also in life. You will find that there are few things better than being a part of a team sport like football. That scrawny kid that will never score a touchdown or maybe even make a tackle, can actually teach his teammates more about life and humanity than you can imagine. The emotions kids feel when an underdog succeeds is a lesson that will stay with them forever. These lessons of teamwork can be the cornerstone to so many great things in other areas of life.

In football, when you have true teamwork, it is like a family. That's what successful football teams become...they become families. And unfortunately in our world today, there's not enough family unity, there's broken homes, there's a lot of tragedy in the world and a lot of people don't ever get to experience family. And sometimes with young men on football teams it's the only family they had. The team is a family and kids consider themselves as brothers. That's one of the things we get from Texas high school football is that family atmosphere. Family means you're pulling to the same direction, you love each other, you may have flaws, you make jokes during tough times, but you're family.

In nature there's so much family. African elephants, when the babies are young, travel in groups always. When they see lions come around, the African elephants herd the babies into the middle of the group and then they face the outside...the mature elephants...the adult elephants face the outside and stare at the lions. The babies are in the inside, the lions can't get to the baby elephants. It's such a demonstration of family; those elephants are saying "You want our babies? Alright come get them because we're butt to butt and you're gonna have to go through us to get them."

And that's the way it is with the football team, we get butt to butt and we say "This is what we are gonna do. You just try to stop us." That type of mentality that we teach in football is so crucial to be successful in life.

As in the wild, so too on the football team. Each team member must perform their task to make the team successful. Eleven men, working together can achieve much more than the sum of their whole. People who work together will win. Individual commitment to a group effort - that is what makes a team work, a company work, a society work, a civilization work. When you are in the work force whether it be a struggling startup or Fortune 500 company, teams make everything happen. When you are in a relationship, it is a team. We are social creatures designed to work together to accomplish things greater than we could on our own. The entire history of the human race is created by teams.

Hannibal didn't cross the Alps by himself. Hitler wasn't defeated by one superstar who was faster or could jump higher than everyone else. Neil Armstrong's walk on the moon required the works of tens of thousands on a team. Even Jesus didn't spread his gospel by himself.

ACCOUNTABILITY

"A man's word is his bond. If a man agrees to do something than he is honor bound to do it, no matter how inconvenient. A hand shake is more binding than words on a piece of paper."
-Hub McCan - Second Hand Lions

If the backbone of a team is teamwork, then the core of teamwork is accountability. Having accountability changes you from just another person, to someone others can count on. They can count on you to do what you say you are going to and most importantly, to tell the truth. These days, accountability is becoming rare in our leaders. We have politicians claiming they didn't do things when the evidence is clear that they did. When our leaders tell us one thing and do another, it trickles down to society. How many times have you heard, "yeah, we should get together sometime," when both of you know it is not going to happen? That is a lack of accountability and that is not acceptable in Texas high school football.

"This is how it works in football, and in life, if you don't have enough confidence to bet on you – on you personally – then don't walk in that huddle. And if the other 10 guys in the huddle feel like that guy can't bet on himself, and he won't give his all for me, don't allow him in the huddle."

"I don't want to walk into a huddle questioning the guy my left, or to my right. I don't want to question the guy. Not only on the field, but also what he does off the field. One thing about a team, is we know everyone's business. We know how guys prepare, we know the guys in the weight room, we know the guys that go to class and don't go to class, we know the guys that are accountable."

"This is a game of accountability. Accountability and availability. Don't tell me about talent. God gave you your talent men. It's a gift from God. Don't you waste it. But here's the deal. When you walk into the huddle do you trust each other? Because the coach ain't in there."
-Herm Edwards

Coach Purcell told his kids in Denton that if you do something wrong, one of the strongest demonstrations of strength is to admit that you're wrong. Some people won't admit that they're wrong. He told his head coaches to be accountable, look people in the eye and say, "You know... we made a mistake on that."

That's what accountability is, being accountable for your actions because your actions affect other people. And so be man enough to look people in the eye and say you screwed up when you screw up. In football, there is no room (or allowances made) for those who shift blame to others or avoid taking a stand. If you drop a pass, you have to own it. Complaining that your opponent is holding you when you are blitzing the quarterback is not how you solve a problem. Sure, you can explain it to others but just saying it won't solve it. You need to own the fact that you didn't get past him, modify your approach and do something that will succeed.

DECISION MAKING

In Texas high school football the quarterback steps up under center, looks over the defense and makes a decision. Should he keep the ball on the option? Should he hand it off? Does he see something else that requires him to call an audible and change the play altogether? The offensive linemen have to make decisions. Are we gonna zone block this or do we need to man block? The wide receiver has to make a decision to change his route. The running back makes a split-second decision if he cuts to the right or cuts to the left.

"Split-second decision-making sets winners apart from losers."
— Stephen Richards

The nature of this game requires us to make decisions and it's a great learning ground for future life. This goes beyond the players. It is a great training ground for young coaches as well. You have got 25 seconds to call a play. You really don't even have 25 seconds, because the play has to be signaled into the huddle in time for them to relay it all 11 players. Then you get sacked and you have to analyze what happened, why it happened, how to avoid it, oh... and you are running out of time to call the next play. This game is chess on crack!

Those are the obvious instances of decision-making but there are a ton of others and every single one builds on a person's ability to make decisions outside of football. It is through the repeated practice of decision making that you gain knowledge. They say you learn good judgment from experience and a lot of that judgment comes from *bad* judgment. You learn from your mistakes and you move on. A mistake is only a negative if you fail to gain knowledge from it.

If a player tries playing football the next morning after going out drinking with friends, he learns that his stamina is reduced as a result of the night before. The player learns respect for his body and that knowledge informs his decision the next time that opportunity (trap) comes up.

Let's break down what decision making really is, why it is important and how football helps build those decision making muscles. When faced with a decision, your brain goes through a few key steps. In football, each of these steps are often handled in fractions of a second.

1. **Recognizing there is a decision needed:** A ball carrier is approached by a defender intent on tackling him.
2. **Analysis of the situation:** If the doesn't take action, he will likely be tackled.
3. **Analysis of the options:** Should he cut left... cut right... hurdle the tackler?
4. **Choosing the best option:** His training and experience will allow him to choose wisely.
5. **Taking action:** Taking decisive action and learning from the choice are paramount. The only thing harder than knowing the right thing to do is to take that action.

"A problem well defined is a problem half solved"
-- John Dewey

The ability to make wise decisions quickly is a skill. This skill is honed on the practice field and in games. Each time the athlete exercises that skill, he improves his ability, just as with any other skill. Earlier in this book, how a person reacts in a stressful situation was given as an example of poise. A large part of having poise is the ability to make decisions in a stressful situation. Again, the need to be decisive in a highly charged situation makes the lessons learned that much more ingrained in the athlete. In a more relaxed setting, the learning isn't nearly as hard-wired.

The practice field is where most of the decision making skill is learned. Through tackling drills, tip drills, blocking drills and all the other repetitive drills associated with football, that decision making skill is continually developed. The coaching staff being on hand to debrief an athlete after a choice makes the lesson even stickier. Whether through positive reassurance that they made a good choice or pointing out the mistakes, that quick feedback reinforces effective decision making.

How the coach communicates with the athlete is a critical factor in decision making. When a coach reinforces a self-awareness in the athlete, they are doing much more than simple positive or negative feedback. A good coach will explain the the choice an athlete faced and get them to be aware of why they made the choice. This self-awareness is critical in developing effective decision making skills. This develops an athlete's internal communication and that is the core of good decision making.

Taken to the next level, the decision making learned in the arena of football directly impacts an athlete throughout his adult life. When faced with a mental crossroads in the future, a former athlete will have a much easier time making decisions because that skill was developed and strengthened. Deciding whether to rent or buy, speed through a yellow light or slow down, or even go jogging or have another piece of pie is so much easier after having faced a third and long, down by 6 with 35 yards to go and 3 seconds left on the clock.

LEADERSHIP

Leadership is one of the most misunderstood concepts. There are many out there who think of a stern taskmaster when they think of a leader. In the realm of football, they think of a thick-necked, angry man blowing his whistle and criticizing players. That is not leadership.

Leadership is just that... leading people. It is not demanding people to do things. It is not sitting in your office and barking orders. It is inspiring people to follow you in order that they can grow and become the best version of themselves and that together, everyone can accomplish more. One of the most overlooked aspects of football is how it develops leadership in the participants.

In order for a team to work as a unit, they have to have direction. Yes, the coaches make the decisions that affect the obvious things... when to punt and when to go for it. When to substitute one player for another. When to slow down and burn the clock or hurry up to beat it. But, players get involved in those decisions and much more.

It is a subtle thing to watch a young man that has never led anyone begin to step up and lead his teammates. You see it in all aspects of Texas high school football:

- When he chooses to run hard during drills
- When he encourages others by cheering them on
- When he picks up trash on the field or in the locker room
- When he dresses nice for team functions

- When he helps a teammate to his feet
- When he asks questions that show he takes the game serious
- When he takes things seriously
- When he lightens the mood
- When he shows up on time or early
- When he corrects teammates showing poor behavior
- When he says "Yes, Sir" and Yes, Ma'am"
- When he goes to the front of the line if volunteers are needed
- When he leads.

"We all need people in our lives who raise our standards, remind us of our essential purpose, and challenge us to become the-best-version-of-ourselves."
-- Matthew Kelly

When someone steps into the role of leader, it changes him and it changes the people around him. Taking on the mantle of leader is a big responsibility and the main reason why so few take the job.

Anyone can be a leader. You don't have to be older, stronger, faster or smarter than anyone else. You just have to have a desire to be a better person every chance you get and help others to do the same.

Some kids will step up and take on that role easily and will continually show leadership qualities. Anyone however, can take steps to lead in hundreds of different situations. It will not always be the same person leading the way. One day, it could be the offensive lineman busting his hump on wind sprints that causes everyone to take notice. Another time it could be the 3rd string tight end getting fired up and cheering on teammates. Or perhaps it could be the linebacker who says something funny right after his defensive back and wide-receiver get into an argument. And most assuredly, it is when the whole team shows up at school event wearing their ties or clearing the tables after lunch.

"A player who makes a team great is better than a great player."
-- John Wooden

One of the things that leaders do is to keep enthusiasm alive. Whether you are in the midst of a 50 game winning streak or haven't won a game in two seasons, it is hard to get enthusiastic each and every week. Coaches, and the leaders they develop, take responsibility to fan the flame of enthusiasm to keep it going.

> *"No one keeps up his enthusiasm automatically. Enthusiasm must be nourished with new actions, new aspirations, new efforts, new vision. Compete with yourself; set your teeth and dive into the job of breaking your own record. It is one's own fault if his enthusiasm is gone; he has failed to feed it."*
> -- Papyrus

It's great to be on top; it's great to have those rings. But if you want to really prove yourself, stay there... stay on top... find a way to just stay there. Then you really created a legacy for your team, your kids, your community and everyone involved with your program. Leaders are constantly working to keep those fires stoked. The more leaders a team has, the better the team will be. When this happens, the individuals improve, the team improves and the entire program improves. These learned leadership skills will also carry them to greater success after football is finished.

FOR NEW COACHES

One of the best things about Texas high school football is the strength of the coaching brotherhood. With over 100 years of coaching across several thousand schools, there is a ton of experience. One huge benefit of that experience is how open this brotherhood is when it comes to sharing what they know... not only about the game, but about the profession.

Here are some of the lessons that experienced coaches share with young coaches:

1 - You never get it all. You can have the best mentors in the world that seem to know everything about the sport and the profession but rest assured, if they have been around awhile they are still learning. It is that habit of lifelong learning that has gotten those guys to the top. Any coach that thinks he knows it all, isn't long for this profession. The game is ever-evolving and with that comes not only new Xs and Os but opportunities to bring back and tweak philosophies and strategies that may have been dated just a few years earlier. Understand that you will never know all the answers and make a commitment to continue learning and you are well on your way to a successful career.

2 - Don't be a YES man. When you are just starting out, it can be easy to fall into the trap of wanting to please your head coach by agreeing with everything he says. You weren't hired to parrot his thoughts. You were hired to bring your talents, knowledge and work to the position... with that comes opinions. Pay attention however to how veteran staff members approach sharing their opinions. There is a right way and a wrong way to interject or even disagree with your head coach.

3 - Do the work. The first thing you need to understand if you plan to last a long time in coaching - at least in Texas, is that NOTHING is below you. It is that commitment to doing the little things that will get you noticed (and appreciated) the fastest. Whether it is striping the fields for a soccer game (even if you have no involvement in that sport) or picking up some trash in the locker room, the best motto is, "if it needs to be done, I'll do it." When you are seen as someone who gives first, you are a valuable addition to any team.

4 - Networking is vital. Chances are you already understand this because not many people get hired in Texas high school football by just sending in a resume. Chances are that your first, next and last job will be given to you by someone you met. Some of the best places are the annual meetings. The Texas High School Coaches Association (THSCA) Coaching School is the gold standard of events where you can learn a great deal about the profession and meet coaches who will play an important role in your career. If you stay at home waiting for a phone call, it isn't going to happen. You have to put yourself in front of people. Make sure to follow up and keep in touch with an occasional phone call or text too.

5 - It's not about the Xs and Os. More important than whether you run the slot-T, a spread or the veer, is how you teach it and get the "buy in" from your staff and athletes. Many, many coaches run similar or even identical offensive and defensive systems with a huge difference in results. You can write off a year or two of success as the difference in athletes but what about those consistently good programs? They are consistently good for a host of reasons, but the biggest factor is that their coaching staff educates well, motivates well and gets the kids to believe in what they are selling.

6 - Don't make it about the money. You hear about the college and NFL coaches making millions each year in salary and think, "I can do that." If you got into coaching for the money, you may have a very short run. Just like the pee wee football player with dreams of playing the NFL, that dream is such a small percentage chance that to focus on that, will almost guarantee you to come up short. One of the great things about Texas high school football though, is that coaching is a profession here and not just a hobby. That said, entry level jobs and even head coaching positions at some districts do not pay monetarily a fraction of the value of the time you will put in. Yes, if you work hard and do well, you can make a good living coaching football. But, retiring to private island is not in the cards. This profession is a calling and when you are in your calling, money is a side effect, not the goal.

7 - You can't win by yourself. Just as we teach our kids that it takes everyone on the team doing their job to win a football game, so too in the coaching profession. When it comes time to build your staff, remember that you don't want those YES men warned about earlier. Remember that you need people willing to do the little things and stay late... to counsel a kid when needed. Remember you need a school that is *bought into* the program and supports your efforts. You need administrators that have your back when things come up (and they will.) You need parents who understand the program and work to support your efforts. You also need the support and faith of your kids.

8 - Remember who helped you. As you progress in your career, the worst mistake you can make is to start believing it was all your own doing. You were put in a situation through thousands of machinations of people you met, conversations you had, players who bought into your system, administrators who backed you, parents who helped you in ways you never even saw, family that supported you and a Heavenly Father that made it all possible. If you forget this for even a moment, you do all those who helped you a huge disservice.

9 - Pay it forward. The coaching fraternity will be at the core of many of your best friendships. Not only will you make great friends but that assistant coach you met in your first stop could end up being your boss in your next. Just as you were helped along in your path, it is your responsibility to help someone else climb their ladder. When there is someone in your program that jumps to do things without being told or even asked, you need to do all you can to help that person succeed.

And most importantly...

10 - It's about the kids. You may have started your coaching career with dreams of winning a state championship, teaching the world a new game plan you designed or retiring as the all-time winningest coach in high school history. Heck, it may have just been about coaching your former high school team to victory over your arch rival. In the end though, if you are going to succeed it needs to be about the kids. Even if you started out with selfish goals, if you stay in it long enough, those goals will fade and you will come to understand that in helping young men become adults of character, you are developing greatness in yourself that no stadium named in your honor can touch.

FOR PARENTS

Parents, this doesn't mean that if you sign your kid up for football your work is done. In fact, it is the handing over of parental responsibilities that have made football so important in society. Yes, it is one of the last places left where young athletes can learn so many life lessons, but your job as a parent can greatly increase the chance of these lessons sinking in. By *working with* instead of *deferring to* the coach and football program, you can make all the difference.

Here are some steps you can take as a parent to ensure kids get the biggest benefit from playing football and other sports:

Behavior after a win/loss. Do not treat your children different based on whether they perform well and win or perform poorly and/or lose. Yes, intellectually your kid knows you love him unconditionally. He knows that you want the best for him, but when a parent gets highly charged up after a win or can't let go of a loss, it can send him a different message entirely. The last thing you want is for a child to believe their value is dependent on whether they win or lose a game. They need to know that you are steadfast and your love for them doesn't falter.

Winning is not where the lessons are taught. There are more lessons taught during losses or periods of struggle than ever learned because of a win. It is your job as parent to support your child 100% during a win and 100% during a loss. The struggle is the journey... winning a district title or state championship ring is not.

Behavior on the sidelines. It is so tempting to shout out instructions from the sidelines and to justify it as "being a passionate fan" or "heck, I would do that even if my kids weren't involved." During the game, your child needs to concentrate on the voice of his coach, the officials and his teammates. Adding your screams to the mix of what to do, where to stand, etc., just confuses him. In addition, it is embarrassing and distracting to your child. All it serves to do is likely to make his performance worse.

Badmouthing. There is never a good reason to badmouth anyone. Nothing is to be gained. If you talk bad about the coach, you teach your kid to undermine his authority and doubt his word. This can destroy everything him and/or the sport has taught him. If you badmouth the refs about a bad call or something unfair, you teach your kid to look for excuses. The call either happened or it didn't - badmouthing the call doesn't change the call.

Keep your emotions in check. Yes, it is good to be an exuberant fan. Yes, it is good to show your support for the team. No, it is not good to be bat-shit crazy. It is not good to be a spectacle. Doing so will only succeed in taking away from the performances on the field and making *you* the performance. In addition, it send the entire wrong message. Maintaining composure is a lesson that can help your son throughout life. There will be ups and downs in life just as in football and for him to be able to handle them, he needs role models that do so.

It is his experience - support it, but don't take it. How you communicate this is simply what pronouns you use. "We" had a heck of a game or "we" finally got that play to work the way it was drawn up. This is an easy trap to fall into because you tell yourself that you are being inclusive and are a part of the experience. Again, be supportive of his experience but let it remain his.

Align your goals. This is one of the toughest ones for parents to do. Often times, your goals as a parent are completely different than that of your young athlete. You want him to get a scholarship or make all-district, win a state title... but he wants to play and have fun. He may have some of those same goals but often times, they are put in his head by you, the parent.

That is not to say that you shouldn't strive for things like scholarships and it is a fine line between sharing with your child the possibility of him earning a scholarship and pressuring him to do so. Frank conversations with him that are not aimed at directing his focus but educating him work the best. Again, it is absolutely okay to have big goals... just make sure they are his goals.

Here are some thing to understand as parents:

Football stinks. Okay, the sport itself is amazing, but *playing* it causes a lot of odor. It is an opportunity however to reinforce some fundamentals about bathing, grooming, picking up nasty clothes and by the time they are in high school - actually learning how to do laundry. You will be thankful for that bit of advice.

You won't be yourself. There will be times when it feels like an alien has taken over your body. You will catch yourself doing things like encouraging Johnny to "play through the pain" or maybe encourage him if he is sick to suit up and try because after all, it IS the playoffs. I'm not saying you will endanger your child, but if some tape or ibuprofen will get him back in the game, you'll be on board.

You will forget it should be fun. There will be times when you are tempted to or just outright put more stock in how your kid plays instead of whether or not they had fun. You will know better as you are doing it, but as a fan of the team and your son will find yourself in that situation. When you do, acknowledge it, correct it and move on.

You will learn too. Just as your child will learn that it is not all about winning, you too will gain a better understanding that sometimes the greatest lessons are learned on the losing end of the score.

You will learn about physiology. You will be introduced to a level of understanding about the human body and its pains that you never imagined.

You will celebrate. When his team wins or he does well, you will high five and give him joyous hugs.

You will give support. When his team loses or he does poorly, you will give long comforting hugs.

You will be spending holidays and birthdays at a hotel. The best part is that you will feel grateful for being able to play football on Thanksgiving or Christmas weekend because it means your child is on a winning team.

You will blame the coach and/or referee. You may feel bad about doing so later... but not too bad.

You will appear schizophrenic. You will go back and forth between sheer joy over his sports involvement and utter disdain for it.

You will learn about his teammates. You will see who is a slacker and who gives his all... and learn that is often not the most talented player.

You will develop new friends. Your circle will include people you never would have encountered any other way and you will cheer right alongside them.

You will have irrational hatreds. Yes, that nearby town you used to think of as a nice place to visit will become home to your bitter enemies.

You will miss things. When he makes that great play you may be looking down to answer a text.

You will learn about your child. You will discover his belief system, things that motivate him and things that get him down at a whole new level.

You will judge other parents. You will decide if they are doing it right or not.

You will become THAT parent. You will seemingly always be talking about how your son did in practice or the game. You will find opportunities to bring it up at the strangest times.

You will love the young man that develops. You won't love him any more than you would have had he not played, but you will appreciate the affect that this game and those coaches have had on him.

You will miss it. After they have gone off to college/gotten married/moved away, you will look back at these days and wish you could touch those feelings again.

FOR ATHLETES

Everything in this book is actually for the student athlete. The information contained in this section however, is a step-by-step guide to a few thing that will help you to:

1. Be a good football player
2. Be a good man
3. Succeed in life

Some of you may be thinking, "yeah, I'll work hard and be a nice guy, but I won't succeed because I am not a gifted athlete." Whether you are the first string star quarterback or the absolute slowest and weakest member of your team there are things you can do that require absolutely no talent. (refer back to WHY FOOTBALL?) They are all within your control and if you master them, you will always have a spot on any team worth its salt.

Coaches have to evaluate every single player on the team regardless of your ability to run, pass, catch, block or tackle. What they need to know:

- Are you coachable? Do you take instruction? Can a coach count on you to do a task when a game is on the line? Being ready to step in and do what is asked will make you invaluable to the coaching staff
- Are you trustworthy? Do you do what you say you are going

78

to or do you miss practices and film study? Can a coach count on you to take initiative and put in extra effort?

- Do you have a good attitude? Will you be a positive influence on the team or a distraction? Will you arrive ready to work?
- How do you act when no one is watching? Nothing reveals character more than what you do when no one is watching or for those who cannot help you.
- What motivates you? Are you fired up by team goals or are you only concerned about collecting your personal newspaper clippings and stats?
- Do your teammates like you? The strength of a team is directly related to how much a player trusts and respects the man next to him. If you don't do that, a coach cannot count on your teammates to have your back when needed.
- Do you understand the game? A player that has a good grasp of all the aspects of the game can be counted on to fill in for other positions or at least will give a coach confidence that you understand the instructions given you.
- Do you want to be here? Motivation is much easier when dealing with players that genuinely enjoy the game. If you have that enthusiasm, it not only makes playing the sport a ton of fun but it will be contagious and spread to your teammates
- What are your strengths and weaknesses? For a coach to help you improve he needs to understand where you have room to grow and where you are maxed out. It not only helps him create a stronger team, but it helps make sure you are in a position where you have the best chance of success.
- How do you respond to problems? A coach watches closely how you respond after a mistake. Your body language (slumped shoulders, pouting, temper tantrums, head shaking) screams in silence. When you own the mistake and come back wide-eyed and focused on the next rep, it tells a coach a lot about his ability to depend on you when things get tough.
- How you handle success & praise? When you score a touchdown or make the game-saving tackle, you will be praised. Do you showboat, gloat and make it all about you or do you thank people politely while pointing out that it was a team effort?

These judgments are made every single day about every single player and the accumulated data is what tells a coach if he can depend on you, how far others will follow you, how far he can push you, what situations it is safe to put you in and what piece of his puzzle you will fulfill.

Now, ignore this list. This is not about a cheat sheet or crib notes. It is about becoming the best version of yourself and that isn't done with a numbered list. It is accomplished by doing the work. Re-read the book and really adopt each of the values spelled out as part of your core being.

Notes on Social Media

Chris Doelle wrote a book about social media as it relates to student athletes, "_Student-Athlete Social Media Playbook: What Every Coach & Athletic Director Needs to Know About Social Media._" While the book is aimed at coaches and administrators and how they can help to keep their athletes and programs out of social media trouble, it is full of useful information for athletes too.

Here are few things coaches look for in your social media postings:

How you treat people Do you show that you truly love and respect those around you? Are all your pictures and messages about how you are going to be a superstar in the NFL or do you have pics of your dog, your grandma on her birthday? Do you treat your opponents with respect? Do you trash talk? There is nothing wrong with saying you're going to win a game, but keep it classy. Do you look like a fun person to hang around or some punk that tries to pose looking "hard" or too cool to bother?

What you consider important Are your tweets all about your new shoes, girls and cars? Do you share videos of workouts or twerking? Do you talk about coverages or making fake IDs? Are you positive and motivational or do you just bitch about things that aren't to your liking?

How you use free time Are you tweeting 100 times a day? Do your

80

Instagram stories go on and on? Do you prioritize the things that will get you places in life or just things that make you look good?

How you use and interact on social media is a window into you as a person. You may think only your friends are watching, but rest assured - your coaches, parents, community and definitely college recruiters are watching too. Don't be stupid.

SUMMARY

If we are only teaching kids to kick a ball, catch a ball and throw a ball, we are wasting a lot of money. But if we're teaching Texas high school football players discipline, pride, poise, class and accountability for your actions and decision making skills, then think of what a better world we've made when those kids get out in real world. That's what it's all about.

One of the important lessons that Texas high school football players learn is that life is not fair. Coaches point that out by showing that football is not fair. Sure, there are rules in place to try to keep it fair, but in the end it really isn't. Sometimes you have to face up against a team that is much better than yours. That is not fair. Sometimes the ball bounces right through your hands into the opponent's. That is not fair. What about injuries? You make a cut as your shoe slips out from under you and sprain an ankle. Where is the fairness in that? Or the wind kicking up right as your kicker has the ball heading toward a field goal? Nothing fair about that. Every year in Texas there are games canceled from lightning strikes in the area or even the occasional hurricane. That certainly isn't fair. None of this even mentions the times when a bad call was made by an official or a player gets away with an illegal action. Anyone who thinks football is fair, is just plain wrong.

In learning that, they learn that as adults there will be times when things are not fair either. There will be times when you're running late for work only to find you have a flat tire. Maybe you're the best teller at the bank and your plan is to work your way into a management position and eventually Vice-President. But the bank President's son graduates with a business degree and walks right into that VP job. He's the vice president now and you worked for 15 years for that position and life's not fair. No, life is not fair. That isn't important. What *is* important is what you do about it. How do you respond? How do you handle disappointment?

In high school football, when we hit on a negative situation you've got two choices. You either respond or you react. Usually reaction is negative. You should have been the starting running back - he just joined the team. It was unfair they won because we lost two starting linemen... that's reaction.

Response is - I just have to work hard and prove that he made a mistake and I deserve that job. We just have to regroup... bad things happen to good people. We talk about that over and over in football... you don't let the unfairness define you. You don't make excuses and you don't blame others. Things might not be fair but we face the reality of what has happened and make a plan to deal with it.

Football teaches players they can overcome problems and can still function when something unfair happens. They can build the mental muscles required to both overcome and learn from adversity they encounter along the road to achieving their goals. Learning to overcome and keep moving forward is a mental skill that will serve them well for the rest of their lives.

It is much more though...

Former Texas high school football players will take so much more than just the great values laid out in this book. They will also take a thousand memories. They will be memories of shared struggle. They will be memories of personal, team and school pride. They will touch every emotion and burn into the minds of the players.

Some of the things that stick with players forever

- Putting on your helmet the very first time
- The heat of two-a-days
- That play - we all have one we remember vividly
- That game that was colder than any other
- The bus rides after road games

- The pep rallies
- Winning that game you weren't supposed to
- Losing the one you shouldn't have
- The friendships built on the practice field
- That drill you hated more than any of the others
- The one you kinda liked doing
- The feeling of accomplishment
- The feeling that you failed
- Knowing someone special was watching the game
- The day you realized it was all over

Coach Ken Purcell and Chris Doelle are 17 years apart in age but when they met for the first time, none of that mattered. The Brotherhood of Texas High School football is one that instantly connects men around the state. It is the shared experience... the shared philosophies and values that erase differences in age, race, income, education, religion and vocation. These differences are ignored as this fraternity of men whose lives were changed by Texas high school football are instantly brothers when the question, "Where did you play football?" comes up.

This is a small fraction of the things that will stick with former Texas high school football players. One of the questions asked of former Texas high school football players when they sign up for **The Brotherhood of Texas High School Football** is, *What is your favorite thing about your Texas high school football career?*" Here are some of their responses:

"Coach Jon Tate was the most influential man outside my dad when I was growing up." **Michael Copeland**, OL/S - Clyde class of 1965

"The friendships it developed. I still talk to a lot of those guys, even today...and breaking some Crockett kid's glasses when I tackled him along the sideline (that was pretty cool)." **Glen Lewis**, LB - Austin Bowie class of 1994

"Ronnie Gage was my most influential coach. My favorite line he used was , "There's no substitute for hard work." **Kris Hogan**, QB - Grapevine Faith Christian class of 1992

"The most influential coach was Neal Wilson my head coach. I played for him in high school, worked for him as an assistant, and later he hired me to be the head coach at Lewisville High School. A 43 year association with Coach. He is the reason I have been coaching for 35 years. Tremendous man, motivator, and coach." **Ronnie Gage**, C/S - Decatur class of 1971

"The relationships I built with my teammates and coaches." **Jeff Ables**, QB - Crockett class of 1980

"Coach Hatcher as my JV coach @ Boswell during my Sophomore year said to me when I moved up to Varsity during two-a-days, 'dont get to comfortable up there.' That has motivated me never to be satisfied and always work hard." **Sean Densmore**, OL/DE - Fort Worth Boswell class of 1994

"Playing the game I love beside my brothers under the Friday night lights!" **Gary Proffitt**, QB - Goldthwaite class of 2001

"The legendary Bill Bryant coached me my freshman and sophomore year. He gave hope to a little guy that never touched the field. I went on to have a decent career at Stephen F. Austin University only because he saw something in me. I was later named the AD/Head football coach at Center High school and Coach Bryant was the first person to call and congratulate me." **Kevin Goodwin**, WR/CB - Center class of 1992

"High school football taught me how valuable "Teamwork" is in success. It carried over to my career in the United States Navy where it was on display through out the Persian Gulf/Iraq War." **James Osburn**, TE - Vanderbilt Industrial class of 1984

"The most influential coach has to be Coach David Evans. I really enjoyed playing for that guy. I was very fortunate to learn the game from him. He was always willing to listen to me, even if it was not football related. He was the one that made sure I

found a place to play, even though I could never find a position to call home. As an adult I used him has a reference and he has shared an interest of what little success that I have achieved." **Justin Simmons**, - Donna High School class of 2003

"Nothing prepares a man for the real world like football!" **Jim Billo**, DE - Goliad class of 1975

"The fun of competing. The sportsmanship and camaraderie that takes place. Beating Llano four years!" **Billy Don Everett**, QB/RB - San Saba class of 1957

"Coach Clyde Evatt believed in me." **Andy Hawari**, LB - Cisco class of 1979

"At the time I didn't realize how special it was but now that I am older I realize that I was fortunate to be part of a special game. My favorite thing about my high school career was the special bond we had as a team and all my high school coaches. " **Jake Escobar**, WR/DB - Comanche class of 1991

"My life was forever impacted by head coach Fred Jackson and defensive coordinator George Boles." **Mark Pool**, DL - Henderson class of 1973

"My favorite thing about playing for Everman was our commitment to excellence. No matter what, in football or life, we had to give our best." **Isaac Sturges**, OL/DL - Everman class of 2002

"Playing for the Panther Nation & my father, John Outlaw" **Stephen Outlaw**, WR - Lufkin class of 2000

"It taught me hard work pays off. I am the only on in my family to ever graduate college and I owe all that to the people that were part of my high school team." **Ron Davis**, DE - Cypress Creek class of 1992

"Not being the biggest, strongest, or fastest player on the field and still doing work." **Kevin Velez**, LB - El Paso Del Valle class of 2012

"I have to say that all my coaches were awesome and great influences on not only myself but my teammates as well...Coaches Bren Holland, Mickey Mitchell, Larry Hanna, Doug Roarke, & Max Johnson." **Rudy Sotelo**, DE/WR - Monahans class of 1970

"Coach Paul Gips" **Andy Pate**, OL/DL - Refugio class of 1952

"I'm just thankful I had the opportunity be apart of something special, but I can definitely say it was truly a rewarding experience and that I met some lifelong friends while playing there. I really would like to thank all of my coaches while I was there for working with me; every single one of them were extremely instrumental to my growth and development as a man and will never forget their teachings." **Martese Henry**, QB - Dallas Skyline class of 1996

"Too many stories to tell regarding the football games, however many thanks to my past coaches and one who changed my life forever Glenn Hill." **John Buffa**, CB - Spring Westfield class of 1987

"My offensive line coach - Coach Gerald Meyer had the greatest influence on my life to be the best that I could be both on and off the field! Taught me grades were more important than athletics and that education will be what puts "bread on the table!" He influenced me so much that I got into the educational field in my college major and in fact Coach Meyer hired me for my first teacher/coaching position in Denison , Texas that led me to a 34 year career in the state of Texas educational system! THANK YOU Coach Meyer for your influence on my life!" **Jim Kazmierski**, OL/DL - Pasadena South Houston class of 1964

"The memories that were made have been even sweeter to enjoy and share over the years." **Dale Zerr**, RB/OL/LB - D'Hanis class of 1988

"When I smell cut grass it reminds me of practice. We got tired of being beat by Brownwood in those days and thanks to Coach Art Briles, we got them back in 90's. Go Jackets!" **Tommy Shelton**, RB/CB - Stephenville class of 1978

"Playing with the guys I grew up with and playing for coaches who really cared about you. I am in my 35th year of coaching high school football and wouldn't trade what I do for anything." **Don Clayton**, QB/P - Nederland class of 1975

"My coaches that taught me how to be a good man!" **Brad Turner**, QB - Weatherford class of 1984

Longtime University of Texas Head Football Coach Mack Brown tells this story about University of Texas Hall of Famer, 3 time All-Conference player in the Big 12 and Dallas Cowboys Pro Bowl wide receiver Roy Williams:

"We're getting ready to play Texas A&M and the media says 'Roy, is this the biggest game you've ever played?' He said, 'No, no no. I was at Odessa Permian when we played Midland High, that was a much bigger game than Texas A&M vs Texas!'"

These comments left by Brotherhood members are just a tiny sampling of the great stories they tell when they think back to their Texas high school football days. More often than not, the favorite thing recited by former players is not about a play, a trophy or a championship... its about the lessons learned on and off the field thanks to the great coaches and great tradition that is Texas high school football.

Note From the Author: Reviews are gold to authors and really helps our books get

CLASS

"Class is an aura of confidence that is being sure without being cocky. Class has nothing to do with money. Class never runs scared. It is self-discipline and self-knowledge. It's the sure-footedness that comes with having proved you can meet life."
-- Ann Landers

First let's define what class is. It is style, manners, intelligence, the people you surround yourself with, the books you read, the movies you watch, how you handle either good or bad events. But is it more than that. It is is treating everyone with dignity and respect regardless of your relationship with them. Class is working to be the best you can and doing the best you can for yourself and others.

"Class never tries to build itself up by tearing others down."
-- Rudyard Kipling

Great football coaches teach class and make it an integral part of their program. Really, the game of football, with the smashing of bodies together at high speed, teaches class? This book isn't about just what is learned in the act of playing football. This is another area where coaches teach by example.

Athletes are taught class while playing football not only through the obvious things - helping an opponent up after a tackle or retrieving the ball and bringing it to the referee after in incomplete pass out of bounds. It also teaches class through literally thousands of acts of kindness a player witnesses in and around the game.

- A coach that lends an ear to a student (even if he/she is not on the team)
- A player that pulls a younger one aside to help with his technique
- The students that show up on Saturday morning to clean the stadium
- The car that honks and waves as they pass the bus on the way to a road game
- The football parents who run the concession booth at games
- The treats left for the players in their lockers
- Friends and family lined up along the road to cheer the bus as it heads out to a playoff game
- The players visiting the elementary school to high-five the kids
- Booster club fundraising events like auctions or "meet the team" nights
- A post-game hug that is just as long and tight whether it was a win or a loss

It is much more than those outward things. Players receive daily reminders that they have the great privilege of playing a sport they love, and with that comes a responsibility to live up to and honor the game. As a player you are taught to give back to your community. You are taught that people look up to you, not because it is so special to be a football player. Instead, they look up to you because you take on the duty of being a role model and kindness is a big part of that.

Texas high school football programs are very high on service. Community service. School service. Service to your teammates. It is very important to build teamwork and to build class in an organization. Whether you are helping your community or helping a teammate, it is always rewarding. Often times the reward is far greater for the one delivering service than for the receiver. Take the time to volunteer and help your community.

"Unexpected, undeserved, unrewarded acts of human kindness change lives ... every time. Their effects are undeniable."
-- Bill Curry

"Yes, Sir" and "Yes, Ma'am" are not about showing someone else that you are in any way "less than" them. It is not about deferring to their superiority. It is simply about respect. This is one of the values that has been diminishing in society and is nearly extinct. It is however, alive and well in Texas high school football. If you think it is corny or old-fashioned, you are welcome to that opinion. Just understand you are wrong.

Texas high school football coaches teach players to respect others and be kind. They teach kids to hold the door for someone (especially a lady) and to say "thank you", "you're welcome" and "please." In some schools, the Varsity football players even remain back in the cafeteria after lunch to clean up the area after the lunch period. It is not seen as corny, old-fashioned nor demeaning. It is a great example of performing a kindness for others. Performing an act of kindness is a sign of class.

In an interview on Lone Star Gridiron, Coach Purcell tells this story of class, "Class as I described to my kids is win, lose, or draw we walk across the field, we shake hands with the opponent, we look them in the eye and we say 'good job.' And if we got beat, we still do that. We say 'good job.' We're going to have class in everything we do, the way we dress, the way we get on and off the bus."

"I won a district championship one time in Denison, Texas and we ate at a little steak house. My kids were loading on the charter bus after we ate, and I was up there making sure that the coordinator paid the bill right. The manager walked up to me."

He said "Coach I need to tell you something about your team."
I said "Yes Sir?"
The manager said, "Your kids did not mess up my bathrooms. They didn't get the salt and pepper and loosen the tops. We have had teams that come in here and almost destroyed our place.

He added, "I know you won a district championship tonight, I just want to tell you that you got a great group of kids".

Well, that's Chapter 1 of the story. Chapter 2 is I went immediately to the charter bus and stepped on the bus. My kids know that when the coach steps on the bus they quiet down. But I said, "Guys I wanna tell you that you did something great tonight."

And of course they were thinking about the district championship and I told them "Look out the window of this bus and see that man in there? Let me tell you what he just told me about you," and I repeated what he told me.

I said "You've done two great things, you won a district championship and you also showed me great class tonight."

Examples of class are even more evident when players or coaches are on the losing side of the scoreboard. Sure, everyone is upset when they lose and happy when they win. But the mature ones show class in victory or defeat. That is a major theme taught by Texas high school football coaches. We have all seen reports and videos of coaches losing their cool when things don't go well. (Some of you are old enough to remember Indiana basketball coach Bobby Knight or tennis player John McEnroe.) Those stories make the news, but you don't see things like that often in the world of Texas high school football. When they do, they are dealt with swiftly.

If a coach loses his cool, how can he expect his players to show class? He can't. Things go poorly for both teams in every single game. What separates the classy programs from the average ones is how they deal with these missteps. Classy players don't blame others for mistakes. They don't use dirty tactics to "get back" at opponents who beat them on a previous play. They acknowledge they were beat and determine to do better. They often even congratulate their opponent for a good move.

Football provides many situations coaches can use as opportunities to teach and reinforce their lessons about class.

in front of more people! If you've enjoyed this book, would you consider rating it and reviewing it on www.Amazon.com?

RESOURCES

Here is a list of resources related to Texas high school football

Websites

Lone Star Gridiron
The Brotherhood of Texas High School Football
University Interscholastic League
Texas High School Coaches Association
Texas Association of Sports Officials
Texas High School Athletic Directors Association

Books

As fans of Texas high school football, you will love these books:

The Junction Boys
Twelve Mighty Orphans
Friday Night Heroes
Texas Schoolboy Football
The Kids Got it Right
Friday Night Lights

Other Books by Chris Doelle
Student-Athlete Social Media Playbook
Lame Jokes Rule
Escaping a Manipulative Relationship

Podcasts

Texas High School Football Coaches Show

Learned from Coach - Doelle/Purcell

Lone Star Gridiron Show

OUR GIFTS TO YOU

Thank you so much for taking the time to share with us and enjoy our passion for Texas high school football. As a small way to show our gratitude we have a couple gifts for you:

Sign up to our exclusive newsletter and get access to our book signing and LIVE appearance schedule, speaking calendar, and a sample of Chris' upcoming book *Brotherhood Stories* for FREE. You can sign up here.

As a supporter of Texas high school football with your purchase of this book, we want to give a discounted subscription rate for Lone Star Gridiron. All the news, stories, videos, interviews, stats & history! Regularly $120/yr, your price is less than half of that $55/yr You can sign up here.

Did you or someone you know play Texas high school football? Sign up for The Brotherhood and be listed on your football team's website. You can sign up here.